TODD SAUNDERS

TODD SAUNDERS

NEW
NORTHERN
HOUSES

Dominic Bradbury

280 illustrations

INTRODUCTION

'Saunders' work is modern, original and sculptural, but it is – importantly – deeply in tune with the landscape.

— DOMINIC BRADBURY

Overview

Much of architect Todd Saunders' work over recent years has been focused upon his two homelands, Canada and Norway, and other northern countries. In some respects these distant territories on either side of the Atlantic are worlds apart yet, as one begins to look more closely, many similarities start to reveal themselves, born of their latitudes and landscapes. Canada and Norway have similar climates, with extreme variations between summer and winter, while their topographies also have much in common with one another. These are territories where the mountains meet the water and the sea, with their islands, inlets and fjords playing an important part in the history, culture and traditions of both places. These multiple links may help to explain overlaps in the architecture of these northern regions and also the way in which both Canada and Norway have pulled upon Saunders' heartstrings.

As Saunders himself has suggested, there is a process of cross-fertilization between the architecture of the country where he was born and his adopted country, where he eventually settled down and established his own architectural practice. Influenced by their climates and culture, there are clear and common themes that connect Canadian and Norwegian vernacular architecture, in particular. There is, for example, a tradition of fishermen's huts and boathouses, often raised above the waterline on piers and stilts. There is also the strong presence of farmhouses, barns and farmsteads, made of local materials such as timber and stone. Another important thread is the shared ideal of the summer cabin, often situated by the water or a lakeside, which one might compare and contrast with the idea of a winter refuge, or hut, high up in the hills or mountains. All of these typologies, and others, have resonance in both Canada and Norway, and they inevitably inhabit the imaginations of architects such as Saunders.

For Saunders, these vernacular influences are embedded in his background and referenced lightly and implicitly rather than obviously or explicitly. Saunders' architectural approach is, after all, decidedly 21st century, drawing equally, if not more so, upon Modernist and contemporary architectural principles, themes and ideas. But what binds all of these points of reference together within, as Saunders puts it, 'a dance between the past and the future', is a particular focus on context and a marked sensitivity to landscape, along with the intrinsic beauty of the natural world.

Saunders' work is modern, original and sculptural, but it is – importantly – deeply in tune with the landscape, as this book will suggest throughout. Each of his buildings is an individual response to a particular sense of place, with its own topography, weather patterns, climate, views and vistas, as well as a unique cultural context, whether that might be Bergen or Fogo Island. This positive preoccupation with the landscape, along with a fresh approach to site-responsive architecture, is one of the most essential elements of Saunders' work, wherever it might be. It is a thoughtful concern, tied to an awareness of environmental responsibility, which lends Saunders' portfolio a sense of cohesion and character, resulting in houses and homes that are not only resonant and deeply distinctive but also gentle in terms of their imprint and impact upon the land.

> **My Dad's side of the family were all furniture makers … my mother's side of the family they were all carpenters … one way or another, design and making were kind of in me from the start.**
>
> — TODD SAUNDERS

Background

Before Todd Saunders eventually made the decision to settle in the Norwegian city of Bergen, which is now his home, he lived in a handful of different countries. Each of these experiences, from childhood onwards, clearly played an important part in the evolution of his thinking and his approach to architecture and design in general. And, like any good story, there were essentially three chapters to this complex and multi-layered journey, encompassing Canada, Europe and Scandinavia.

Saunders grew up next door to the 'crossroads of the world'. Gander International Airport, where his father worked as an aeroplane mechanic for Air Canada, was a key fuelling stop for transatlantic flights during the fifties in an age just before long-haul passenger jets. It was used by most of the major mid-century airlines, including Aeroflot flights from Moscow to Cuba. Saunders and his family lived in a prefab house, put together by his father, in the town that grew up alongside the airport, which sits within an area of flatlands on the island of Newfoundland.

'I would spend one or two days a week with my Dad at the airport as a child,' says Saunders, 'and he would call us up and say Clint Eastwood or the Rolling Stones are here for a stopover, and we would get on our bikes and go over and see all these stars. I remember the smell of Cuban cigars and it was fascinating seeing the Cuban pilots and stewardesses, who looked like they came from another planet.

'My Dad's side of the family were all furniture makers or builders and he was someone who could fix anything. He would also take a chance on things and was always finding out about something new, so we had these weird cars and motorcycles. On my mother's side of the family they were all carpenters and they could all draw really well. So, one way or another, design and making were kind of in me from the start.'

One of the first buildings to make a big impression on Saunders as a child was the family's own lakeside summer cabin. As a ten-year-old, Saunders helped his father and uncle build this simple timber structure, which was both remote and off-grid, with no electricity or phone line. Saunders, his mother and two brothers would spend the entire summer up at the cabin, even after his father's own vacation had ended and he was back at work.

'My Dad would fly up with a pilot and check up on us,' Saunders says. 'If there was anything wrong, we had this fire all ready to burn and if we needed help then we'd set it alight and my Dad would know that he needed to come and get us. I was helping and watching and learning while they built that cabin, and by the end of it I probably knew enough to start my own architectural practice. It was all self-taught and, in a way, my whole career has been part of this long autodidactic process. I'm not afraid of learning by doing something, and I think that comes from growing up getting used to being dependant on your own skills.'

Later, when Air Canada stopped using Gander as a hub, the family moved on to Halifax, Nova Scotia, where Saunders went to high school and eventually, after a foray into maths and science, to art school. He began studying Environmental Town Planning, including a semester at the Rhode Island School of Design on an exchange programme. Following on from graduation, and greatly assisted by free airline tickets through his father's job, Saunders headed off to Europe looking for work, experience and inspiration.

He began in Vienna, working with the Austrian landscape architect Maria Auböck for the summer. From there, Saunders stepped onto a train and headed to Berlin, where he found a job with Hans Loidl, a landscape architect and professor at the city's Technical University. This was followed by some time back in Canada working with another influential landscape architect, Jane Durante, based in Vancouver.

'One of the reasons for working with these different practices was that I wanted to understand the lifestyles of these architects and the ways in which they worked and ran their offices,' says Saunders. 'I also wanted to dig deeper into ecological architecture, and it was Jane Durante who told me that I should be an architect rather than going down the landscape route and that I should go to McGill University in Montreal, so that's where I did my masters. After my first year I managed to get two research scholarships that took me back to Europe.'

The subject of Saunders' research was the ecological villages of Northern Europe, a thesis that eventually led him to Bergen. Hitch-hiking most of the way, his extended trip through Germany, Holland, Denmark, Sweden, Finland and Norway saw Saunders arrive in the city and almost instantly fall in love with the place:

'I felt really at home straight away because it was like Newfoundland. There were the mountains, kayaking, mountain biking and great architecture. I went to an outdoor restaurant, drank a beer and the sun was shining and I decided that one day I would come back and live here. I was only here for a few hours on that first trip but eighteen months later I was back and living in Bergen.'

Practice

Saunders' years of travelling, working and studying in Europe helped to focus his interest on ecological and sustainable architecture in particular, while also playing an important part in formulating his ideas about what kind of practice he wanted to create for himself. Time spent working on the evolution and development of two eco-communities, one near Trondheim and the other two hours north of the Russian city of St Petersburg, also fed into his thinking.

By the time he settled in Bergen, after completing his master's thesis for McGill, Saunders knew that he did not want to be part of a large architectural machine and that he needed the creative freedom to pursue his own passion for a unique kind of responsive architecture that operated in close synergy with the landscape. The decision to stay in Norway, rather than pursuing job offers elsewhere, seemed very natural.

'In a way, I stumbled on a place that looked like Canada and responded positively to it,' says Saunders. 'But it was a lot more than that. The Scandinavian lifestyle is different from Canada's in some ways and they know the value of solitude, of rituals and traditions. They really appreciate all of these values in Norway.

'There are connections with food, agriculture, fishing and all sorts of things, but also connections between vernacular architecture and contemporary design. It's architecture that is built to last and it's very pared down with no fuss. There's a simplicity to it that I respect and the skills I learned in Newfoundland are easily transferable to Norway and vice versa. There are parts of each society that I like and some that I don't, but given the way that my life fits into these different places I have everything I need. What I don't find in Scandinavia I can find in Canada and it works the other way round.'

Committing himself to a new life in Norway, Saunders worked with a Bergen practice for a few months before forming a partnership with a like-minded Norwegian architect, Tommie Wilhelmsen, who is now based in Stavanger. Starting from scratch at the age of twenty-six, Saunders devoted all of his time and energy to building up the practice, securing clients, learning Norwegian and refining his approach to architecture, as well as teaching at the Bergen School of Architecture, which is where he was introduced to Wilhelmsen.

'Tommie and I got along really well right away,' says Saunders. 'We had the same interests, a similar sense of humour and we were both very hard-working. A lot of other architects around us were always talking about what they were going to do one day, but we knew that we just had to get on with it. We built this little cabin together and then won a competition for the Aurland Lookout and suddenly we had credibility. We were renegades but we got some attention locally and then nationally and then internationally.

'We only had a short time together as "Saunders & Wilhelmsen", working on three buildings over the course of two years, but we designed about thirty projects together. I think if we had continued working together than we would have burned each other out by the time we were forty, because we were working so hard and we just put our hearts and souls into it. But we are still good friends today and we ended on a good note. Working with Tommie, I learned that sometimes you need to take a chance and now I am almost fearless but not careless. Taking risks used to be like jumping into cold water but now it's second nature.'

Soon after arriving in Bergen, Saunders had begun forging links with local carpenters, builders and artisans and spending time in the workshop developing ideas and prototypes. This collaborative way of working continued and became increasingly important as he established his own eponymous practice. Even now, when the workload is increasingly international, Saunders has kept his own

Top right – Hytte Tyin is a modern cabin situated on the edge of Jotunheimen National Park, Norway; the house was designed to be in tune with the landscape and the sloping topography of the site.

Middle right – Todd Saunders' Tower Studio, one of six artists' studios commissioned by the Fogo Island Arts Corporation, on Fogo Island, Newfoundland, Canada.

Bottom right – Saunders' Hardanger Retreat, a modestly scaled escape overlooking Hardangerfjord in western Norway; this off-grid cabin was designed in conjunction with former associate Tommie Wilhelmsen.

studio relatively small while developing an extensive network of friends and colleagues across Norway and Scandinavia, as well as Canada and North America. It's a combination of the micro and the macro, with Saunders balancing hands-on time in the workshop and a creative dialogue with collaborative partners, including project architects, surveyors, technicians and interior designers (see Ways of Working, page 123). Such an arrangement allows Saunders to remain focused on the design process itself, rather than devoting time to managing a large atelier, with all the logistical challenges that this brings.

'I don't really identify myself that much with other practices, because we do work in this very individual way,' says Saunders. 'There are other Canadian and Scandinavian architects I admire, like Shim-Sutcliffe in Canada, Reiulf Ramstad in Oslo and the Finnish architect Sami Rintala. But I have never wanted a big office full of staff because it's much too restrictive in terms of creativity and the kind of lifestyle that I have. I want to be able to spend time up at my cabin experimenting with new ideas, or with the carpenters in the workshop, and I want to ski, mountain-bike, go kayaking and be with my family.

'There is a tradition here and in Canada of living in nature and using that as a way of recharging. Those ties between architecture, nature and the landscape are really important to me and they build on each other. So the opportunity to have some solitude and to think is easier here than in other parts of the world. The practice is busy, but I also need to take time to concentrate on the creative side, which is what gives me energy. It's the same for musicians and writers in Norway and Canada: the solitude, the remoteness and connecting with nature all help to foster the creative process.'

New Northern Architecture

Since launching the practice in 2002, Todd Saunders has balanced residential and non-residential projects, with each part of the portfolio helping to enrich the other. One of his first completed commissions was Villa Storingavika, a substantial family residence in Bergen. A 'labour of love', the villa was – characteristically – the result of a close collaboration with the clients and the gradual evolution of a design tailored to the needs of the family as well as the landscape.

Each of Saunders' houses and cabins, many of which are explored in more detail over the pages that follow, is fully bespoke in the sense that it is not only site-specific but also a unique response to the requirements of his clients. Each project has its own context and programme, which develops through discussion as well as research and analysis. Yet there are certain common threads to the work, and a Saunders residence is recognizable as such.

There is, generally, a modesty of scale and a light footprint derived from Saunders' intrinsic respect for the landscape. More substantial houses are often broken down into smaller component parts to reduce the impact of a building upon its setting. Similarly, a number of Saunders' buildings explore the idea of elevation and ways of lifting a structure above the topography to reduce any impact upon it, while landscaping is kept to a minimum.

Fine craftsmanship and detailing are also essential priorities for the practice, adding to the sculptural simplicity of Saunders' work. His buildings are robust and well constructed, generally using steel frames and high standards of insulation, while timber coats give them character, depth and personality, as well as tying them back to

a deep-rooted understanding of the beauty and integrity of natural materials in both the vernacular and Modernist traditions of the northern countries.

Plans and layouts maximize not only natural light, but also vivid connections with the surrounding landscape or coastline. Similarly, outdoor rooms such as integrated terraces and decks maximize the relationship with the surroundings while balancing the need for open and sheltered fresh-air spaces. Inside, there is generally a welcoming informality to open-plan and multi-layered living spaces, yet – on the other hand – the practice appreciates the importance of more intimate and escapist spaces. Saunders talks of the idea of clients rewarding themselves with the 'gift' of a spacious master suite or another kind of personal, favoured space, such as a library or study.

Importantly, Saunders' non-residential work has helped to inspire and influence certain ideas explored within his houses and cabins. The Aurland Lookout and Stokke Forest Stair projects, for example, helped to fine-tune ideas related to architecture and observation, exploring ways of enhancing the experience of connecting with vistas and viewpoints. Saunders' design of the Fogo Island Inn, in Newfoundland, explored the use of stilts and pilotis to elevate the building above the ground plane, a principle also developed in a number of residential projects, such as Salt Spring (see page 56) or Villa Grieg (see page 170). Similarly, Saunders' sequence of modestly scaled artists' studios on Fogo Island has helped to influence approaches to sustainability and off-the-grid living, but also to the development of annexes and satellites for

Top right – The Aurland Lookout, designed in conjunction with Tommie Wilhelmsen, described by Saunders as a 'gangplank' looking out over the striking landscape below.

Middle right – Like the Lookout, the Stokke Forest Stair offers a fresh perspective on nature and the natural world; the realized stairway was delivered to site by helicopter.

Bottom right – Slice, in Haugesund, Norway, is an inventive hybrid fusing indoor and outdoor living spaces, or a studio and terrace, while wrapping itself around the mature trees on the site.

a number of residences, such as Villa Tyssøy (see page 156) and Villa AT (see page 68).

This two-way relationship between the twin sides of Saunders' portfolio also gives rise to hybrids that help to break down the boundaries between typologies. One example might be Saunders' Slice project in Haugesund, which fused the idea of a garden house with a deck, or outdoor room, wrapped around existing mature trees. Slice, along with other studios and annexes developed by the practice, can be used in many different ways, pointing towards fresh structures that can be shaped and moulded by the end-user.

Essentially, as mentioned at the beginning, the narrative thread that ties all of these elements together is environmental responsibility. There is a respect for the landscape that takes us from Saunders' upbringing in Canada, to his research trips exploring eco-communities in Northern Europe, to the range of his work in the northern countries. Across both residential and non-residential projects, the practice is fully committed to site-specific, 21st-century sustainability and buildings that have intrinsic longevity and flexibility.

'As architects, it's really important that we put the environment first,' says Saunders. 'The thing about a landscape like Fogo Island in Newfoundland, or parts of Norway, is that it's not going to forgive you if you destroy it. In some countries the land might repair itself in a few years, but if you destroy a site in Newfoundland it will take hundreds of years to get back to where it was. So, even though these are strong and powerful landscapes, we do have to be very careful.'

'There is a tradition here and in Canada of living in nature and using that as a way of recharging. Those ties between architecture, nature and the landscape are really important to me and they build on each other.

— TODD SAUNDERS

Opposite – The glittering view over Lake Nordås from the central courtyard of Villa Grieg.

HOUSES
— PART ONE

VILLA AUSTEVOLL

Bekkjarvik, Selbjørn
Austevoll, Vestland, Norway

Given the northern climate of Norway and the challenging conditions experienced along its coast, the notion of 'shelter' has particular resonance here. There are the dramatic extremes of the winter, but also the winds from the north and the constant chance of rain any month of the year. One of the key challenges in the design of the island retreat of Villa Austevoll was how to balance the necessity of shelter with the need to make the most of this extraordinary coastal landscape all year round.

'The key element in our minds when we went to see Todd for the first time was that we need shelter,' says Trond Gundersen, who commissioned the house together with his wife, Anne Iren Fagerbakke. 'We want to be able to be outside all the time and the design of the house makes that possible. We have breakfast on one terrace with the sunrise and then we can sit outside at night on another terrace and still find shelter. We are always under cover on the terraces, protected from the wind and the rain.'

The house is situated on the island of Selbjørn, which sits within a picturesque archipelago to the south of Bergen. Accessible only by boat and ferry, Selbjørn is a place that Fagerbakke has known since childhood, when her grandparents lived here and she would come and spend time on the island during the summer months and weekends. The land where Gundersen and Fagerbakke (an engineer and a civil engineer respectively) wanted to build a new escape for themselves and their grown-up children has been in the family for many years.

'I spent time here all the way through my childhood,' says Fagerbakke. 'It's always really beautiful in early to mid-summer, especially in June. At that time of year you get some gorgeous weather and amazing light across the sky. In June, you have light almost all night long and we wanted to feel part of that even when we were inside the new cabin. We wanted a building that would take the light inside so you can see it everywhere.'

The couple approached Saunders to design their new retreat knowing that his ideas would be highly original. They wanted a cabin that would give them shelter as well as an observatory for appreciating the beauty of both land and sea, but at the same time they wanted the house to be unusual, modern and sculptural.

'We saw a boldness in Todd's work,' says Fagerbakke. 'We didn't want something that simply blended into the terrain and disappeared. We liked the way that Todd uses contrasts and draws these forms and shapes on top of the terrain.'

Previous pages – Seen from the water, the relationship between house and setting becomes clear, with the main body of the house floating above ground level while the living-room window and balcony face the fjord.

Opposite – For Saunders, the island and the archipelago reminded him of Newfoundland, with the architect designing the house in response to a unique setting. The original sketches were made on the ferry back to Bergen following the first site visit. Positioning the house correctly was key, requiring careful site analysis and model-making, which included three-dimensional topography.

> "When I first went to the archipelago I thought it was one of the most beautiful places in the world.

— TODD SAUNDERS

Previous pages –
Seen from above,
the form of the villa
becomes clear, with
the circular skylight
over the staircase
sitting at the centre
of an irregular cross.

Left and opposite –
The house respects
the landscape while
working around both
the topography and
the existing trees and
vegetation, seeking
to make the lightest
possible impression
upon the natural
surroundings.

Opposite – Elevating the main storey of the house helps to create a sheltered undercroft around the main entrance, seen clearly from the approach to the villa.

Above and pages 28–31 – The house looks over the treetops across the coast and the open landscape, framed by the building's four 'lenses' facing north, south, east and west.

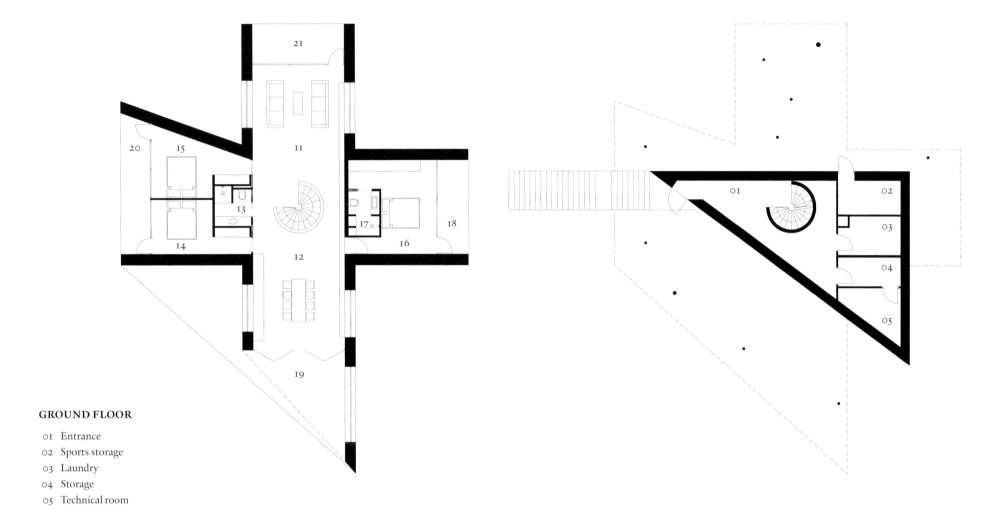

GROUND FLOOR

01 Entrance
02 Sports storage
03 Laundry
04 Storage
05 Technical room

1ST FLOOR

11 Living room
12 Dining room
13 Bathroom
14 Bedroom 1
15 Bedroom 2
16 Bedroom 3
17 Bathroom
18 Terrace 1
19 Terrace 2
20 Terrace 3
21 Terrace 4

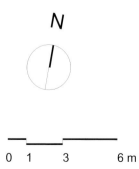

'And we wanted to be challenged,' Gundersen says. 'We were thinking that we would build a cabin here but we wanted to do something different. Todd gave us a concept that made us think, "Yes, this is something else".'

Gundersen had already built the family's main home in Bergen and wanted to be involved in the construction process for Villa Austevoll. He took a trip to Fogo Island to see the hotel and studios designed by Saunders and was struck by the similarities between Newfoundland and Norway in terms of both the landscape and the climate.

'We had done a bit of work together by the time I went to Fogo and it really gave me an understanding of why our house was designed in this way,' Gundersen says. 'It's all about avoiding interfering with nature and it made me even more certain that our house was going to be great.'

Like Saunders' projects on Fogo Island, the design of Villa Austevoll adopts the principle of making the lightest possible impact upon the natural setting and surroundings. Saunders decided to lift the house above the landscape, both to protect it and to take advantage of the hillside site and the views that it offered in all directions. He developed the idea of a cross-like form for the main body of the building, sitting on top of a recessed plinth.

'When I first went to the archipelago I thought it was one of the most beautiful places in the world,' says Saunders. 'To me, the landscape is almost identical to Newfoundland and you can hardly tell the difference. On the way back on the ferry we sketched out the first ideas, and it was all based on the views to the north, south, east and west. We ended up with a perfect cross on a square plinth, but then we started to make some adjustments and variations to the plan. It's almost like pottery where you might have this perfect symmetrical form, and then towards the end you might twist or turn it a little bit as you strive to get the most out of the form.'

Instead of a square supporting plinth, Saunders decided on a triangular slice made of concrete, which recesses into the hillside, while allowing the main body of the floating house above to dominate with its coat of white timber and glass. Slim steel pillars complement the structural, supportive function of the plinth, which contains the entrance to the house. In this respect, the structure can be seen as an evolution of the design of Salt Spring in Canada (see page 56), which is also elevated using a combination of plinth and pilotis.

'It's to do with how the architecture affects the landscape,' Saunders says, 'and that goes back to questions of fear and confidence. Fear of destroying a beautiful landscape that we need to take responsibility for and confidence in the way that you find the right solution, which means that you touch the land lightly. Like Fogo or Salt Spring, the idea is that in three hundred years when we have all gone and the buildings have too, the landscape will still be about the same as it was.'

The triangular plinth holds the entrance hall, utility spaces and a sculptural spiral staircase, crafted in oak, which leads up to the principal level above. Experientially, the journey upwards from a relatively enclosed, darker entry space to a space full of light offering open views of a framed landscape can be compared to the 'promenade architecturale' at Villa Grieg (see page 170).

'The staircase itself is this beautifully crafted jewel, made by Georg Guntern of GG Möbel, who worked on Villa Refsnes (see page 138) and some of our other projects,' says Saunders. 'There is a circular skylight on the roof of the house positioned directly above the staircase, so you are stepping up from this basement area up towards the sunlight.'

The stairway emerges at the central point, an open and welcoming living space arranged on an axial line running from north to south, forming two spokes of the cross. One wing holds the sitting room, including a library wall to one side, while the other hosts the dining area and a fitted galley kitchen. Both of these spaces spill out onto terraces, sheltered by the overhang of the roof. The master bedroom suite in the third spoke and the two bedrooms in the fourth, similarly, connect with terraces facing east and west, so that every point of the cross connects with a key vista. Wind and weather patterns, along with sight lines, influenced the decision to erode the geometry of the cross at crucial points, softening the overall form with more angular elements.

'It might look like a complicated plan but it's actually very simple,' says Saunders. 'Each point of the cross adapts to different weather situations and transforms, so that whatever the weather, the season or the time of day you have a space outside and these four different, controlled views. So, it's almost like a viewfinder with these different lenses looking outwards. The house is very adaptable in the way that a simple box or a circle wouldn't be.'

The steel-framed, larch-clad house was built relatively slowly, taking careful account of the needs of the family and the quality of the detailing and finishes. The couple wanted a house that would combine a cabin-like degree of simplicity within the layout and interiors with relatively low-maintenance materials, taking into account the coastal conditions and the building's hillside position. Given the successful form of the house and its flexibility, the family have found themselves spending more and more time at their 21st-century cabin through all four seasons.

'When we sit on the terraces it's like sitting on top of the trees,' says Fagerbakke. 'It's almost like being in a forest and looking out and we can hear the birds around us.'

'We have started having our morning coffee outside whatever the weather,' says Gundersen. 'There can be some light rain in the morning but the terrace outside our bedroom is usually dry regardless of the weather. We are always protected. Actually, the house looks almost completely the same as the model that Todd built for us at the beginning. We changed two angles but that was about it, and the carpenters really enjoyed building the house. We all had fun with this house. Design should always be fun.'

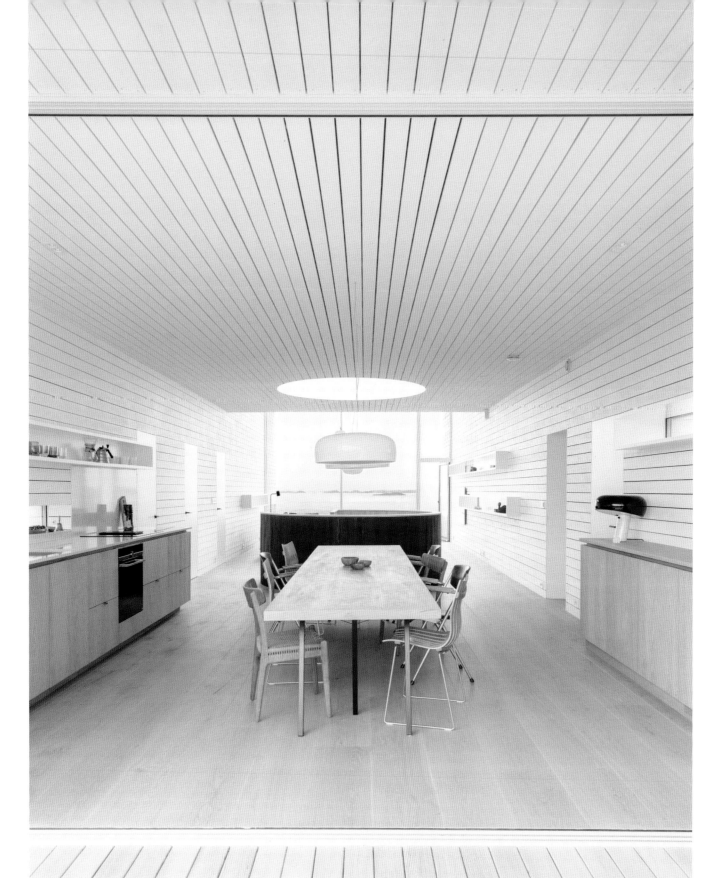

Pages 32–35 – The interiors of the villa have a finely crafted quality, as seen in – for example – the spiral staircase, made in oak by Georg Guntern. The skylight over the staircase offers a natural invitation to step upwards towards the light and into the main living spaces on the upper level.

Left and opposite – The staircase emerges at the centre point between the dining and kitchen area to one side of the house and the seating area at the other. The dark finish on the exterior of the drum makes it stand out as a focal point, contrasting with the white and natural timber used elsewhere. Many elements are integrated, including the kitchen and storage units, allowing the space to remain uncluttered while the balconies become semi-sheltered extensions of the internal living spaces.

Following pages – The master bedroom looks out over the natural landscape; the villa was designed to have minimal disturbance on its surroundings.

VILLA
S+E

Landås, Bergen
Vestland, Norway

Situated in a desirable quarter of Bergen, with views out across the city, Villa S+E was conceived with an unusual but effective strategy in mind to help fund the upkeep of the house and provide its owners with a steady income stream. Just a short tram ride away from Bergen University College's new campus, the lower level of the three-storey hillside villa is devoted to six student apartments and a central communal living area. With its own dedicated entrance and terrace, this part of the house can function independently of the two storeys above, which are devoted to the family's private living spaces.

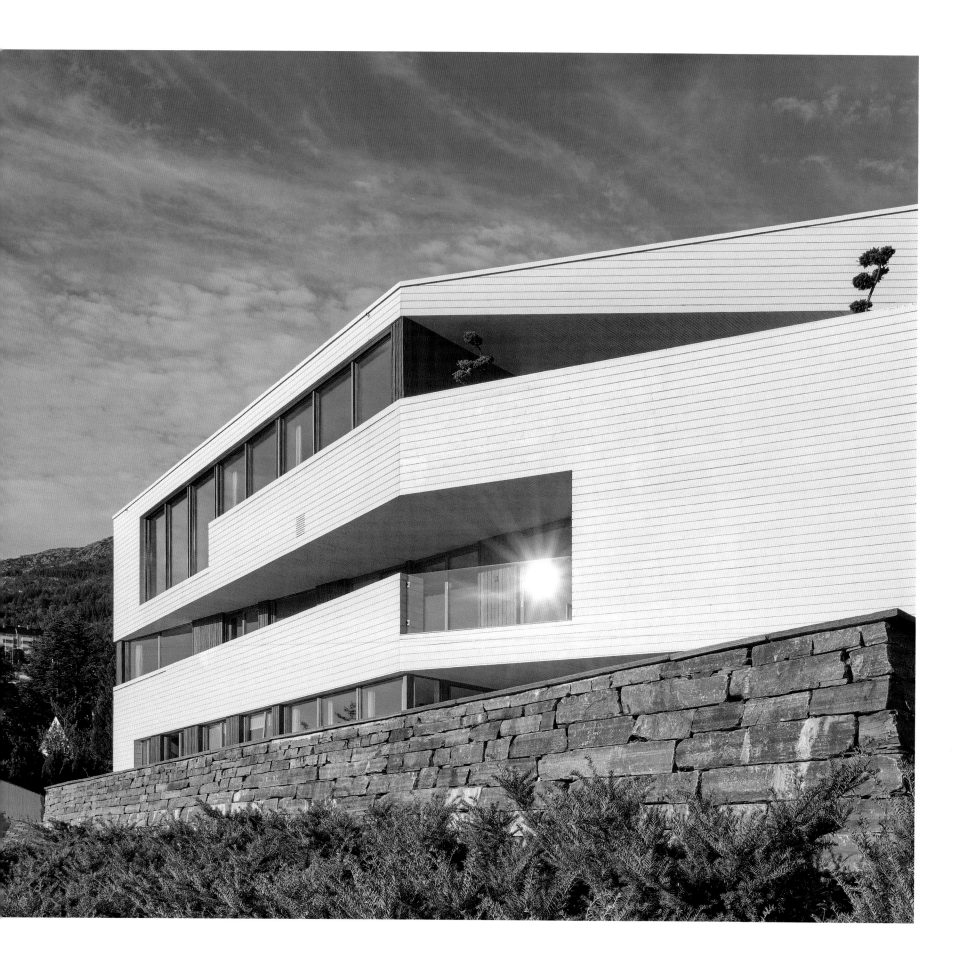

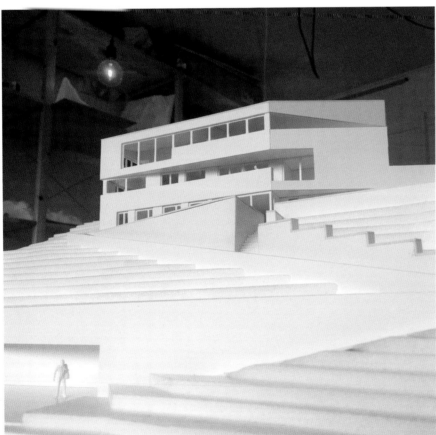

'It's actually a great place to live as a student,' says Todd Saunders. 'They enter from a pathway that runs through the front garden and then, as well as the six bedrooms, there are three bathrooms and a common kitchen, dining and living area at the middle of the plan. The apartments are always rented out because, as soon as someone leaves, then some of their friends want to move straight in. It's a great model for student accommodation but it's also a good model for helping to fund a new family house. Everybody wins.'

The villa was commissioned by surgeon Kari Erichsen and her partner, Hogne Sandanger, a lawyer, who have two children. The couple bought a house dating back to the early 20th century in the Landås region of the city, with the intention of rebuilding. The site itself, which looks down towards Brann Stadium and the college campus (designed by Cubo Arkitekter and HLM Arkitektur) had clear potential, but the existing residence was in a poor condition.

The family initially approached Saunders just as he was about to take a sabbatical in Croatia with his family. As a result, Erichsen and Sandanger spent some time working on ideas with an alternative architect, but they found that none of these plans captured their imaginations. In the end, the family waited for Saunders to return from his sabbatical and began working with him on a fresh design.

'The architects we were working with were not motivated and so we decided that we would ask Todd again,' says Sandanger. 'The design process was a lot quicker, perhaps because Todd had more faith in the project and he quickly came up with five sketches, and the first idea that he showed us was the right one for us because Todd really understood what we wanted. It was very straightforward from that point onwards.'

Saunders gently pushed the house into the hillside, using the student level as a kind of plinth for the family home above. In this respect, the house could be compared to Villa Refsnes (see page 138), which floats above a separate apartment within an older and original portion of the building. Such solutions help to elevate the floors above, maximizing the light and the sense of connection to the open vista across the city.

Three family bedrooms sit at mid-level, along with a reading/media room and a spacious home office, which connects with balconies to the side and the front of the building. Service and storage spaces are all pushed to the rear of the plan, where the house meets the hillside, allowing all the key spaces to enjoy open views to the front, while the fenestration and orientation of the side elevations are carefully planned to ensure privacy from the neighbouring buildings.

Previous pages – Seen from the garden, the three storeys of the villa become clear, along with the stone retaining wall that helps to ground the building to its site. The student accommodation, on the lower level, is accessed via a pathway through the garden and has its own terrace.

Opposite – The final model of the house, made for the construction site, suggests the way in which the house is positioned on the hillside. The villa forms part of a complex ziggurat of homes and gardens layered upon this sloping cityscape, with its views down towards the Brann Stadium below.

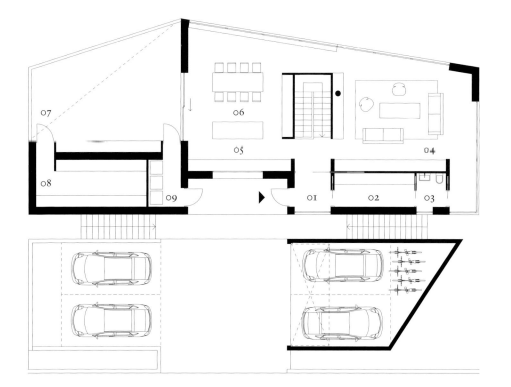

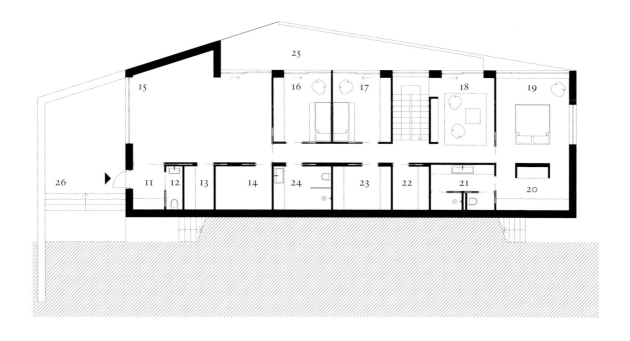

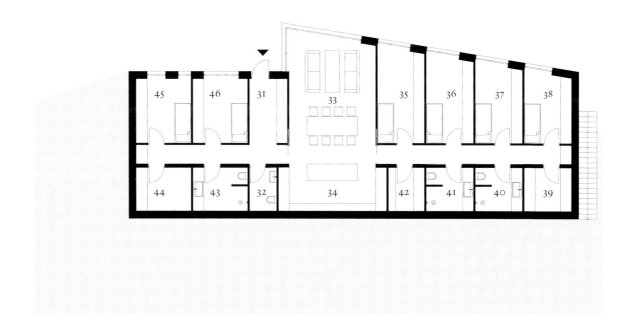

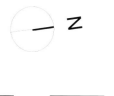

0   1   3   6 m

'We call the line of service spaces to the rear the "thick wall",' says Saunders. 'Finding the backbone of the house really helps us when we are designing a house and the thick-wall theory, where you treat this wall almost like a long piece of furniture, is a way of making sure that the house is very well organized. You can place the bathrooms along that line, along with the laundry, and cupboards where you can store everything away. It's the same principle on the other two floors.'

The design of the upper level naturally makes the most of its elevated position. This part of the house features a largely open-plan living area, but with the crafted timber staircase and its protective surround forming a partial partition between the main seating area to one side and the kitchen and dining area to the other. This highly crafted jewel box also forms an anchor point for the wood-burning stove that warms the spacious lounge. For the interiors, the family turned to designer Eero Koivisto, from the Swedish firm Claesson Koivisto Rune, adding another layer of depth to the key living spaces.

'We felt that they were a good match with Todd's architecture,' says Sandanger. 'They complemented one another and it saved us a lot of time and worry, while resulting in a higher quality for the interiors. So there's no doubt in our minds that it was worth it. Our quality of life is so much better now and when you are working from home, as we have been recently, it's great to have space for the family and a home office. It's the one example I can think of where there is a way that you can actually buy some happiness.'

The upper level features an integrated terrace, which is partially sheltered by the roofline to form a hybrid space somewhere between inside and outside; the main entrance to the house is also on this level, where the building meets the rising gradient of the hill. Much of the exterior cladding is in white timber, punctuated with banks of oak joinery around the entrance area and other key points, such as the more protected portions of the terrace.

'Having these two finishes working together is like a great meal where you have the perfect pairing of food and wine, complementing one another,' says Saunders. 'Everything about the house is extremely well thought out, from the design details all the way through to how the family have come up with a way of helping to finance the house through the student apartments. It's all very smart and all very comfortable.'

Pages 46–47 – Each level of the house, including the student accommodation, has its own outdoor space alongside it, offering a series of outdoor rooms; the terrace on the uppermost level, which adjoins the main living spaces, is partly sheltered, meaning that it can be used even on rainy days.

Right and previous pages – The staircase forms a finely crafted object within the main living area at the top of the house, while also helping to separate the sitting room at one end and the dining area and kitchen at the other; the interiors were designed by Eero Koivisto.

Left – Placing the main living spaces at the top of the house means that these enjoy the best of the views and a rich quality of natural light. The floor-to-ceiling windows frame open views of the city, including Brann Stadium.

Following pages – Seen from a distance, the tiered street pattern becomes clear, as does the way that the new villa sits gently within it; the villa itself was designed to respect the sight lines and privacy of neighbouring houses.

SALT SPRING

Mount Tuam, Salt Spring Island
British Columbia, Canada

Over recent years the idea of a home studio has shifted from a romantic notion to an essential requisite for many of Todd Saunders' clients. The growing ambition to work from home, which has been amplified by the 2020–21 pandemic, has overlapped with the rise of digital technology that makes such an ambition more easily achievable. When Canadian landscape architect Nancy Krieg relocated from England back to British Columbia, she asked Saunders to design not just a house but also a studio that would serve as a fresh base for her work and as a spur to her own creativity.

'What I really love about my home here is that the studio Todd designed for me is a completely separate building,' says Krieg. 'So, psychologically, I feel that I am still going to work. I come out of my house, go across the bridge, open the door of the studio and I'm at work. Then, when I close the door again at the end of the day, I'm finished and I leave work behind and come back to the house.'

Saunders and Krieg first met when they were both approached to contribute to a project for the Durrell Wildlife Conservation Trust, which was founded by the naturalist Gerald Durrell back in the sixties. The project, which was intended for a site on Jersey in the Channel Islands, never went ahead but Saunders and Krieg spent enough time working together to realize that they had much in common beyond their shared Canadian heritage. When Krieg eventually found a picturesque parcel of land on Salt Spring Island, she remembered how well the two of them had connected over the Durrell project.

'When I first met Todd we really got along and that, for me, is just as important as the talent,' says Krieg. 'We do think alike and we worked really well together with Salt Spring, or Vista Falls as I like to call it. The site was marvellous, with the waterfall and the views, so the question was how do you maximize that? How could it all work both inside and outside? When there was a question I would fire it at Todd and he would come back with a better suggestion.'

The site that Krieg had managed to secure was certainly spectacular. The land forms part of a hillside on Mount Tuam, with views out across the Salish Sea, towards Vancouver Island, and to the San Juan Islands, just over the border in Washington State. Part of Mount Tuam itself sits within an ecological reserve, while Krieg's own land has a natural beauty of its own that resonated with both her and with Saunders.

'I went to see the setting with Nancy and there were these giant waterfalls because it was spring and the snow was melting,' Saunders says. 'So, of course, we started talking about Frank Lloyd Wright and there was this joke between us that this was Fallingwater Two, which was the name we put on the initial ideas. But that's how important the landscape was for us. We knew that we needed a house for Nancy and also a studio, so we started playing around with ideas that placed the house on one side of the waterfall and the studio on the other, with a bridge between them. They were almost like two creatures sitting on the hillside and we would move them and shift them around to find out what might work best.'

Previous pages – The Salt Spring house and its separate studio almost disappear among the trees, while creating the lightest possible footprint upon the landscape.

Opposite – Both architect and client saw the preservation of the natural setting as a vital consideration within the project as a whole. Careful mapping and modelling of the hillside site, including the cascading stream, led to the idea of two modest and separate structures linked by a bridge, as suggested by the first study model.

'The design was quite simple, focused on this desk in a big room looking at this amazing vista … It proved that, even in a small space, you can have a whole variety of experiences.

— TODD SAUNDERS

Both architect and client wanted to preserve and protect the site as much as possible, while maximizing the views and the quality of sunlight in both buildings. A dialogue began to develop not only between the two modestly scaled pavilions but also between the buildings and the landscape, including the cascading creek. Saunders began refining plans that meant that no trees would be cut down and also that each steel-framed, cedar-clad structure would float over the hillside, anchored by a combination of slim concrete cores and steel pilotis; the bridge, too, would gravitate above the topography without disturbing it in any way.

'Like Frank Lloyd Wright at Fallingwater, we decided to go down the hillside a little rather than trying to take the top of it,' says Saunders. 'We didn't cut down a single tree and the buildings are really just bolted on to the land. This is one of the first projects where we started thinking about lifting buildings above the land and almost detaching them from the landscape, so that we would minimize any impact on the natural setting.'

The Salt Spring project was Saunders' first completed Canadian commission, yet also coincided with his work on the Fogo Island Inn and the Fogo Island studios, over on the east coast of Canada, where similar concerns and considerations were being carefully taken into account. At Fogo, too, Saunders sought to elevate the architecture so that it sat above the land to help protect it, but also to maximize the relationship with the open views of the island and the coast. More than this, both commissions also involved thinking

about the whole idea of a studio and what it might offer, both functionally and artistically. Saunders has described the Fogo Island studios, many of which are off-grid, as small punctuation marks in an open landscape. The same could be said of Krieg's twin buildings.

'We were really pleased with how the studio turned out,' says Saunders. 'The design was quite simple, focused on this desk in a big room looking at this amazing vista, but it worked really well. It proved that even in a small space you can have a whole variety of experiences. It's got a small kitchenette, a shower room, bookshelves, the wood-burning stove, a terrace and this world-class view from the window.

'The studio is a perfect place for a landscape architect, or a writer or painter, and then if you do have guests they could even use it as a guest room. So it was part of our thinking, along with the Fogo Island studios, about how artists, creative people and freelancers work. But at the same time, Nancy's studio and her house do have this conversation with one another, which was another important part of the plan that we developed.'

The house itself is also compact, helping to further reduce the impact of the two pavilions on the mountainside. This modern cottage is, again, arranged on one level, sits lightly on the hill, and features integrated terraces as well as a covered entrance, or porch. The majority of the internal floor plan is devoted to an open-plan living area, which includes a sitting room, dining area and a galley kitchen arranged against one wall. The only separate

Previous pages – The view southwards from Krieg's desk in front of the studio window is an inspiration in itself, looking out across the islands that punctuate the Salish Sea; the studio also includes a kitchenette, a compact WC and shower room, as well as a fold-out bed, meaning that it can be used as guest accommodation.

Above and opposite – Krieg has coated the floors of the studio with a collection of plans and drawings of the house and studio; the wood-burning stove helps meet the energy needs of the super-insulated building in a sustainable manner.

Pages 64–67 – A foot-bridge over a stream leads to the studio, separating it from the house and helping to create a healthy work-life balance.

spaces are the master bedroom, bathroom and a small additional water closet; there is also a roof terrace on top of the cottage.
As with the studio, the design of the house is largely focused on creating a vivid sense of connection with the landscape.

'In the studio, my favourite spot is my "throne" by my desk, looking out,' says Krieg. 'For the house, in the summer I really love the roof garden. Modern houses can be cold and sterile, but people always tell me how welcoming the house is, with this phenomenal combination of being very simple and modern and warm. It's full of charm and very light. One of the key ambitions was that I wanted sunlight in the house all day long and all year round, so I have something different every season, which most people don't have on this island. When other people might be complaining that it's cold and grey, I can just turn my chair and look at the waterfall and that becomes special.'

For Krieg, looking back over the years since the house and studio were completed in 2010, one of her favourite memories is the very first day that she moved in: 'I just looked out of the window and it all seemed to work,' says Krieg. 'I was amazed by how great it looked. I still get calls from movie studios who are working on futuristic films and saw the building on a website somewhere. They tell me they want to film here in this modern, future-looking building and I'm going, "But it's ten years old." It doesn't surprise me so much now as it did on that first day, but I do love it all.'

bed under the box

○5

○2

○1

○4

○3

N

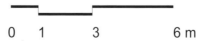

0 1   3   6 m

MAIN FLOOR

01 Covered entrance
02 Studio
03 WC
04 Storage
05 Terrace

VILLA
AT

Søgne, Kristiansand
Norway

For Todd Saunders, the process of designing and building Villa AT offered one of the most rewarding and instructive commissions of recent years. The project provided not only the opportunity for creative collaboration with Saunders' clients and a skilled team of builders and artisans, but also a chance to explore a number of fresh ideas and design solutions. Many of these ideas were only unlocked after Saunders settled on a unique shape and fluid form for the house that worked with the site and the harsh winds that can sometimes affect this part of the southern Norwegian coast.

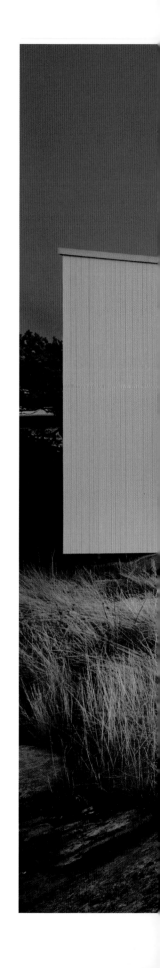

'My clients were always telling me about the wind at Søgne,' says Saunders. 'The view out across the water is amazing but the wind can just ruin the whole day. So we had to make a building with various outdoor spaces and terraces that would be protected from the weather. There's this thing that Norwegians do when they are caught in the mountains when a storm comes in: they dig a hole and get down into it until the storm passes. It was a bit like that with the house. There was this slab of rock in the landscape that you could shelter behind if the wind came up and that helped us to position the house, so that it offered shelter but also connects with the view. One weekend I went into the office and made a little model and that became Villa AT.'

Saunders' clients are a couple (a teacher/singer and an IT specialist) with two children – a son and a daughter. The family already owned a summer cabin at Søgne but were based in Oslo, which is around four hours' drive away. After reflecting upon how much they loved living here on the coast near Kristiansand, they decided to make a permanent move and build a new family home. They came across a magazine article about an earlier residential project by Saunders, known as Villa G, situated by the sea at Hjellestad, near Bergen, and were impressed by the way that the outline of this two-storey

residence had been softened by the use of curving lines and more organic shapes that set the building apart from houses designed with rigid, linear geometries.

The clients decided that they wanted a one-storey home that embraced the sea views, but also asked for a separate apartment for two of their parents. In addition, they were tempted into adding a swimming pool that could be enjoyed by all the family. The idea of a semi-separate annexe for relatives or friends is one that Saunders has explored a number of times over the course of recent projects, including Villa Tyssøy (see page 156). The annexe is set just a few steps away from the main house and is fully self-contained with its own spacious living room, which includes a galley kitchen to one side, plus a double bedroom and a bathroom.

'My wife's parents were wondering if they should get an apartment or exactly what they should do for the future,' says Saunders' client. 'The idea of living in the annexe became a serious suggestion when we got permission to build here. We get along great and it's a very nice arrangement. We have dinner together sometimes but we always knock on each other's doors rather than walking straight in. We don't spend time together every day, but we do now and then.'

Previous pages – The gentle, curving form of Villa AT evolved as a response to the site and setting, but also to the weather conditions, particularly the wind, and the need for sheltered spaces around the house as well as within it.

Opposite – Construction images reveal the steel framework of the new house. Villa AT was designed as a permanent home for a family that had enjoyed spending time at Søgne in their summer cabin, seen by Saunders during the first site visit. The model reveals the relationship between the villa, annexe and pool, along with the way that these three elements relate to the topography.

'The building nestles into the rocks, while a ziggurat of stone steps leads down to the fresh-water swimming pool and pool terrace.

— DOMINIC BRADBURY

The fluid form of the main house was a response to the topography, the weather patterns and the need to frame the views out across the water. The building nestles into the rocks, while a ziggurat of stone steps leads down to the fresh-water swimming pool and pool terrace, which sit within a natural cleft in the landscape. The villa itself is almost Z-shaped, but with a soft, curvaceous outline that could be described as almost Niemeyer-esque. The dynamic façade features banks of curving glass bordered by spruce cladding, finished in a gentle white tone. The use of these curving forms gives the house a marine quality, echoing the waves of the sea below.

Internally, the house is divided into two distinct parts. The family living area is largely open-plan, with only a bespoke, marble-clad fireplace lightly delineating the sitting room from the kitchen and dining area alongside. Oak floors run throughout, while the joinery is bespoke and elegantly detailed, including the kitchen units and the library wall to the rear of the seating zone. A sequence of skylights introduces additional sunlight, ensuring that the space as a whole feels bright and inviting.

There is a natural junction between the two main elements of the house, where Saunders positioned a separate hobby/media room, as well as utility, service and storage spaces

arranged around a well-proportioned and welcoming entry foyer. The other half of the house, beyond this point, is devoted to the family bedrooms. Here, instead of pushing the circulation corridor to the rear, Saunders decided to run the hallway alongside the windows facing the sea view, creating an avenue of light that helps enrich the two children's bedrooms and the master suite at the far end of the line. The master suite consists, in itself, of a collection of both inviting and functional spaces including walk-in wardrobes, the bedroom and the bathroom; both the bed and the cocoon bath are carefully orientated so that they enjoy views of the coastline and sea.

'We really like the open hallway by the bedrooms,' say the clients. 'In classic houses, the hall is usually in the middle of the house or at the back, which means a dark space. But in our house we have the view and plenty of light so we loved that solution. Having everything on one level means that we do use the whole house and it has a good feeling. The design is very graceful and harmonious.'

For both the architect and his clients, the build process was a pleasure, helped by the team of artisans working on the project. A regular dialogue developed during the build between Saunders and the gifted team working on the project,

including builder Øyvind Bakkevold, interior carpenter Stig Drange and designer Hannes Wingate, who collaborated on the interiors, furniture and furnishings, building upon a creative relationship that Saunders and Wingate developed at the architect's own home, Villa S (see page 192). Conversations and video conferences about detailing and finishes led to Saunders regularly sending over additional sketches and notes about, for example, the pattern of the stonework on the terraces and the steps down to the pool, or the hand-planed finish on the oak floors inside the house.

'Given that our studio is in Bergen and the site is down on the south coast, we got used to working closely together at a distance,' says Saunders. 'It was a lot of fun and the local builders and carpenters were like us in that they wouldn't give up until something was as good as it could be. I knew that they were putting their souls into it.'

Architecturally, the combination of a low-slung form that hugs the landscape and the dynamic lines of the façade helps to define the engaging character of this super-contextual home. Villa AT is not only tailored to the needs of its occupants, but to the needs of the site itself.

'The curves came out of being gentle rather than aggressive,' Saunders says. 'The curves don't shout. Like Villa G, it was a question of how you use wood in a "plastic" way. The house becomes an object in the landscape, with just stone, rock and a few trees around it, so we were using what was natural to the site. But from inside, the view is everything. From the kitchen you have a view of the ocean and the living room has a view, as does the master bedroom. When the kids come out of their bedrooms in the morning they look right at the ocean. So the sea has a very big presence all of the time.'

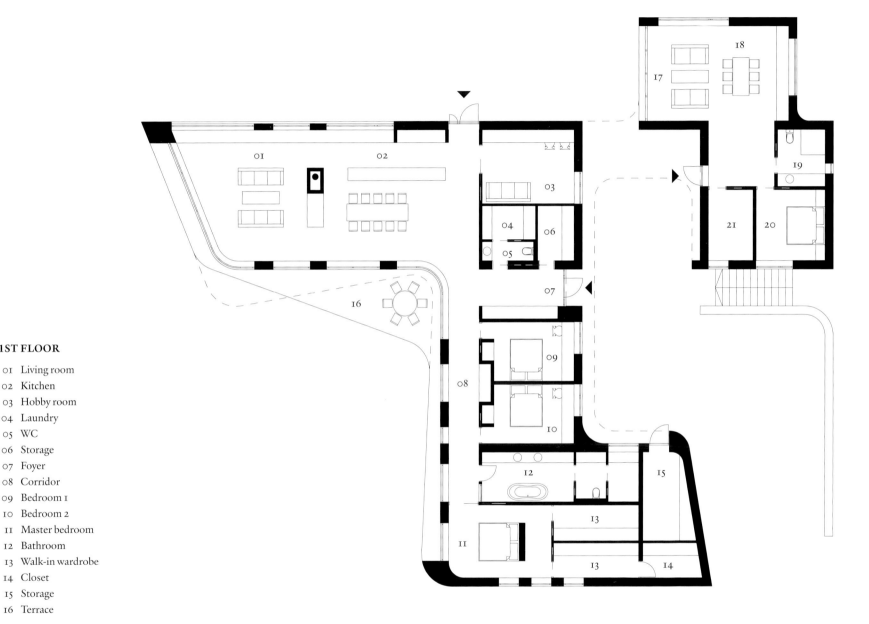

1ST FLOOR

01 Living room
02 Kitchen
03 Hobby room
04 Laundry
05 WC
06 Storage
07 Foyer
08 Corridor
09 Bedroom 1
10 Bedroom 2
11 Master bedroom
12 Bathroom
13 Walk-in wardrobe
14 Closet
15 Storage
16 Terrace

1ST FLOOR ANNEXE

17 Living room
18 Kitchen / Dining
19 WC
20 Bedroom
21 Storage

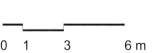

Pages 72–78 – Hugging
the landscape, the house
manages to provide
shelter while also
opening up to the views.
The ribbon of glass
facing the water offers
a powerful connection
with the surroundings,
while introducing a rich
quality of natural light,
reinforced by the use of
skylights.

Left – The main
circulation route is at
the front of the house,
alongside the ribbon of
glass, with the hallway
drawing light into every
part of the house; the
master suite can be
glimpsed through
the open doorway
at the end of the hall.

Opposite – The master
bedroom and bathroom
also benefit from
framed views out across
the coast, with a large
skylight over the bath
tub for a sky vista;
the interiors of the
house were designed
in conjunction with
Hannes Wingate.

Following pages –
The striking living
area has a very slight
cantilever, so it hovers
just above the ground.

LILY
PAD

Lake Rosseau, Muskoka
Ontario, Canada

The vernacular architecture of Muskoka has a distinctive quality of its own. This resort region, around two hours to the north of Toronto, is well known for its picturesque lakes and rivers, bordered by boathouses and cottages that make the most of the surroundings with their porches, decks and terraces. Todd Saunders' Lily Pad house, on the edge of Ontario's Lake Rosseau, offers a 21st-century reinterpretation of Muskoka vernacular fused with a range of Modernist and contemporary influences drawn from North America and Scandinavia.

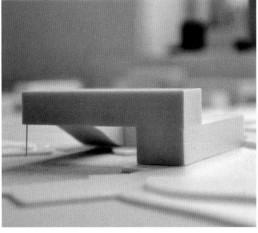

'In Canada, Muskoka Lakes is a little bit like the Hamptons, but it has a real character of its own,' says Saunders. 'You could compare it to the Lake District in England because lots of people from Toronto have summer houses here or come up and spend their vacations around the Lakes. I really love it because it has such a great feeling to it. Artists love it too because the landscape is so beautiful and there's also a strong craft tradition, as you can see with Muskoka wooden boat-building, making these wonderful pleasure boats. My clients wanted somewhere at Muskoka where they could come all year round and a place where family and friends could get together.'

The project was commissioned by a businessman and his wife, who are based in the city but have enjoyed spending time at an island summer cottage in Muskoka for around thirty years. They found a sixteen-acre site on the edge of Lake Rosseau, which connects with Lake Muskoka and Lake Joseph through a network of waterways, and began thinking about building something for themselves that would integrate with the setting but also be decidedly modern.

'We have always been interested in real estate but we'd never built anything of our own from scratch,' say the clients. 'We have renovated houses before but this was the first time that we have built something for ourselves that has our stamp on it. I think it's the culmination of all those years of looking at real estate and it was a project that we were very interested to take on and see how it turned out. We have learned a lot along the way.'

The couple were already thinking about the project when they took a trip to the Fogo Island Inn in Newfoundland, designed by Saunders. Their time on Fogo Island, getting to know the architect's work first hand, convinced them that they should get in touch with Saunders:

'It all started with that trip to Fogo Island. We had read about Fogo many times and really wanted to go, and then as soon as we got back to the city we found Todd's number and called him, and he came to see us three weeks later and we showed him the property. Then the process started, and a few months later Todd brought us a model of the house and the house turned out just like the model. We saw the design and we said this is incredible, so we didn't change the form – we were blown away. We just thought it was very special and different. It was something that really hadn't been built in this area, or anything that looks remotely like this. Now, everybody wants modern.'

'If you have access to the roof, you regain the external footprint of the site that you took away to build the house ... So you don't lose anything, but the building actually gives you a lot more.

— TODD SAUNDERS

Saunders designed a five-bedroom house along with a separate guest lodge, as well as a boathouse on the shore of the lake itself, with Matt Ryan serving as the local architect of record. Both the architect and his clients wanted to maximize the sense of connection with the landscape, while creating a home with a dynamic and original character of its own. Based upon the programme set by the family, the design of Lily Pad explores the idea of elevating the key living spaces to maximize the view while also integrating porches and roof terraces into the form and outline of the building. In some respects, this marked an evolution of themes previously explored in the design of a number of Saunders' recent Norwegian houses, including Villa Grieg (see page 170) and his own house, Villa S (see page 192). But in other respects, particularly the use of the roofscape of the building as another outdoor room, Lily Pad takes the architect's thinking even further.

'I like to think of the roof as a fifth façade,' says Saunders. 'It's something that you see with Adalberto Libera and Curzio Malaparte's Casa Malaparte on Capri [1937], where the roof becomes a terrace, or Sverre Fehn's Glacier Museum in Fjærland in Norway [1991]. It's a way of using all of the surfaces of the building and, if you do have access to the roof, then you are regaining the external footprint of the site that you took away to build the house in the first place. So you don't lose anything, but the building actually gives you a lot more.'

Saunders references the influence of the Muskoka vernacular tradition of outdoor rooms with a lakeside view, as well as mentioning the roof terraces commonly seen in countries such as Morocco, where these elevated rooms are often one of the most tempting spaces in urban riads and town houses. With Lily Pad, the roof terrace becomes the final destination within an ambitious 'promenade architecturale' – somewhat reminiscent of the journey seen at Le Corbusier's iconic Villa Savoye (1931) – that takes you up from the ground plane towards the floating first floor and, finally, to the roof.

There is a choice of circulation routes that take you through the intriguing ribbon-like form of the house as the ground floor twists, turns and ascends as it connects with the upper storey. The imaginative plan of the house also offers a way of bypassing the two internal stairways at ground-floor level. This features the entrance hall and four generously sized bedroom suites, as well as a much-loved media room with tiered seating around the junction between the two storeys. Alternatively, an external stairway at the front of the building provides a more direct link to a substantial, open-plan living space at first-floor level with a sliding bank of glass facing the lake. When the glass slides back, this space becomes – in effect – an enticing open porch, or 'Muskoka room'.

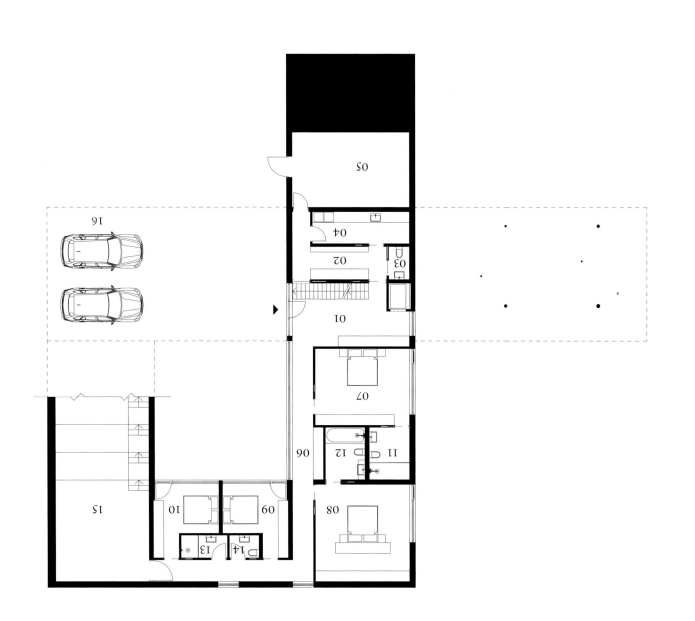

GROUND FLOOR

01 Entrance
02 Wardrobe
03 WC
04 Laundry
05 Technical room
06 Hallway
07 Bedroom 1
08 Bedroom 2
09 Bedroom 3
10 Bedroom 4
11 Bathroom 1
12 Bathroom 2
13 Bathroom 3
14 WC
15 TV room
16 Covered carport

1ST FLOOR

21 Living room
22 Kitchen / Dining
23 Pantry
24 Storage
25 WC
26 Hallway
27 Porch
28 Master bedroom
29 Walk-in wardrobe
30 Bathroom

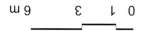

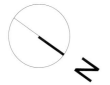

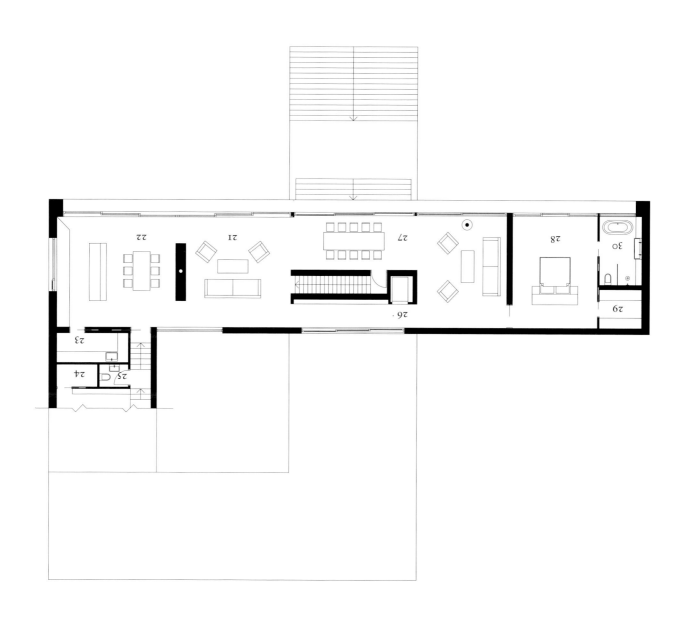

Offering zones for dining and seating arranged around a fireplace, as well as a bar, this is a flexible and fluid space. Although it can be used as a porch all year round, benefitting from this elevated position floating above the landscape, it comes into its own during the summer months. The clients' master suite sits at the far end of the cantilevered bridge that forms the upper storey. Floating beyond the main body of the house, the master bedroom levitates in a dramatic manner, becoming a lookout station facing the lake view to the front.

'With Villa 5, I have a roof terrace and then a library at the top of the building, both of which work really well for me,' says Saunders, who worked on the interiors of the house in collaboration with designers Alex Simpson and Jayme Million of Studio Arthur, who had previously worked with John Tong's Toronto-based design firm, +tongtong. 'But with Lily Pad we wanted a building that you can walk all the way around and over almost every surface. With the family's old house in Muskoka, there was a porch wrapped around it so that you could sit outside or eat outside whenever you liked, and in the summer the only things that you do indoors are cook and sleep.

So with Lily Pad the front of the building on the upper level becomes the porch, which reinterprets their summer cottage, and you can walk straight down this big stairway towards the lake.'

'The house was built and organized pretty much to our way of life,' say the clients, 'so we don't think it will ever change that much. The real beauty of the house is that there is a space for everyone and we're never on top of one another. Everybody can find a space here. I think what we loved at the Fogo Island Inn was the feeling of calm and simplicity, which we wanted to have here, but we also wanted to go for something unique and leave our mark on the planet.

'Being here just makes everyone feel so safe and calm. It's become the safe harbour for everyone in the family. While we only ever used the cottage in the summer, we love being able to come up here whenever we want and at any time of year. It all came out beautifully and we have no regrets. We have been busy this last five years with other things but it has been great to have something else that we were working on that belonged to us. It was our own thing and it was fun.'

The separate guest lodge explores some similar themes and ideas to those exploited in the main house, while forming a private satellite for visiting friends and family. The boathouse, however, has its own distinct identity. While the structure is steel-framed, the exterior of the building is coated in crafted timber, referencing the Muskoka boat-building tradition, with the streamlined profile of its vessels sometimes compared to Italian Riva pleasure craft. A roof deck on top of the boathouse offers another enticing outdoor room, but with a more vivid and direct sense of connection with the lake.

'It's great to see people like my clients still buying locally made Muskoka boats and supporting the industry,' says Saunders. 'They were always asking me about the boathouse, even when we were busy with the main house, so I drew this idea for them. I had been thinking about this while I was using one of their Muskoka boats, so I drew a building with a sloping roof and a stealth-like form with doors at one end opening out to the lake. It's my version of a classic Muskoka boathouse.

'It's about looking back and reinterpreting the past, taking the best pieces of the tradition. With the house, it was the big porch and these outdoor spaces that everyone can enjoy, and then with the boathouse, it was having this "drive-in" building on the edge of the lake, which is part of this amazing Muskoka tradition of buildings with water instead of a floor.'

The combination of these three elements – the main house, guest house and boathouse – creates a welcoming family compound. As in other Saunders projects, breaking the programme down into multiple elements reduces the overall impact of the residence on the surroundings. At the same time, it provides a generous setting for the family to spend time with one another and visiting friends. During the Covid-19 lockdowns of 2020 and 2021, in particular, such an arrangement within an escapist rural setting represented an idyllic alternative to city living.

Left – The detached guest lodge explores some similar themes to the main residence, including elevation, integrated decks and a light touch on the landscape.

Following pages – The stairs that lead to the front of the house draw inspiration from those seen on many historic, lakeside Muskoka homes.

VILLA GRIMSEIDDALEN

Grimseid, Bergen
Norway

There is a thoughtful degree of flexibility woven into the design of Todd Saunders' houses. Importantly, his buildings allow for the possibility of change and adaptation as the needs of his clients gradually shift and alter over time. The concept of 'future-proofing' is particularly important for clients building a family home for the long term. Like many of the families that commission Saunders, the owners of Villa Grimseiddalen, near Bergen, came to him with a commission for a dream home that would fulfil all of their ambitions for the present but also carry them into the future.

'This is a house where the owners can live forever,' says Saunders. 'Generally, Norwegians are not that good at foresight and go with the flow, but many of our clients do think about future-proofing and let it guide them to some degree. A well-designed house should still work through the evolution of the generations. Some of our clients might have an annexe or a "granny flat", but others, like the family at Villa Grimseiddalen, decided on a different plan that gives their teenage children their own space upstairs while the rest of the house is on one level. So it's a house that will still work really well when the children have grown up and leave home, and there won't ever be that feeling of kicking around in an empty house.'

The scale of the villa was an important consideration from the start. The family made a conscious decision to downsize, moving from a larger house to a smaller but fully bespoke building. The setting of Villa Grimseiddalen played a key part in this process, with the family buying a sublime site to the south of Bergen that balances easy access to the city with semi-rural surroundings and an engaging waterside setting. Saunders' client, an entrepreneur who has run his own business for many years, managed to buy an existing cabin here with the intention of replacing it with a new house. Building regulations meant that the fresh building would have to match the footprint of the cabin, which was around half the size of the family's former residence.

'We now have a much more compact house, but we don't miss any of that space,' says the owner of Villa Grimseiddalen. 'Because of the footprint, we were not allowed to build a bigger house but it works fine for us. The other house had a large entrance hall, for instance, and the hallway we have now is smaller, but it works really well for us as we have plenty of coat cupboards and shoe cabinets. We are really happy with the layout of the house.'

The villa sits upon the gentle brow of a hill, overlooking the fjord, with a separate boathouse and a pontoon down at the water's edge. The house has a sculptural and expressive quality, with a mono-pitch roof, grey timber cladding and a bank of glass looking over the open vista. A key element within the design process was the decision to place all of the main living spaces at ground level along with the master suite, while creating a modest upper storey holding the two children's bedrooms and a media room.

"We're always being asked to do flat roofs, but we love the idea of a sloping roof coming down to a point like this, achieving lots of different things in its shape and line.

— TODD SAUNDERS

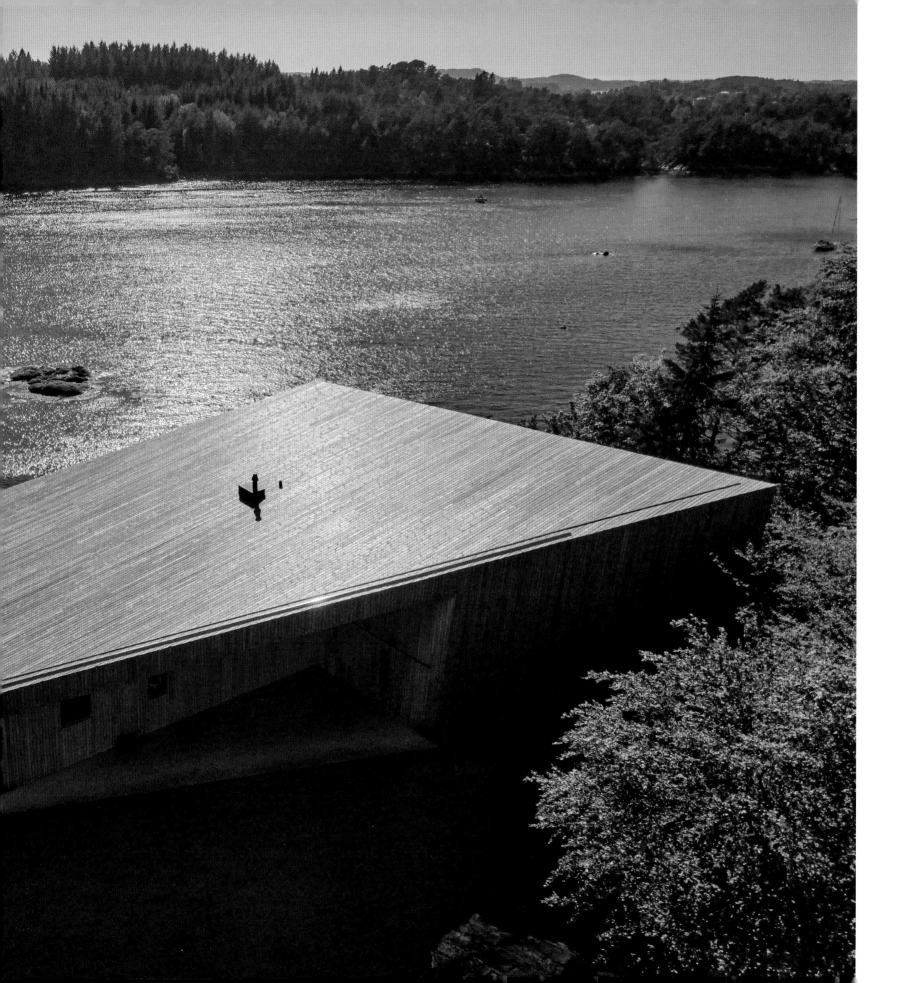

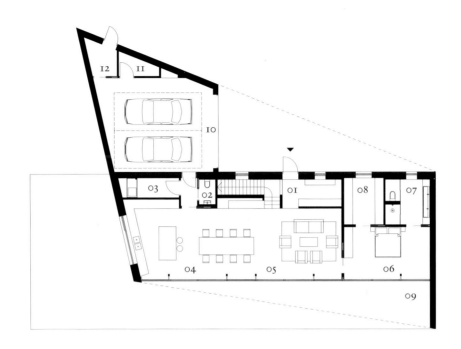

GROUND FLOOR

01 Entrance
02 WC
03 Laundry
04 Kitchen / Dining
05 Living room
06 Master bedroom
07 Bathroom
08 Walk-in wardrobe
09 Terrace
10 Garage
11 Storage
12 Storage

1ST FLOOR

21 TV room
22 Bedroom
23 Bedroom
24 Bathroom
25 Bathroom
26 Storage / Technical room

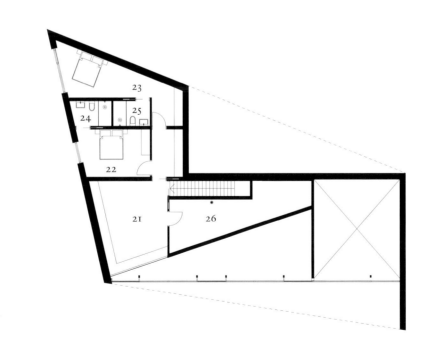

Pages 106–08 –
The sculptural form of the angular roof projects gently outwards at the front of the house, helping to shelter the terrace that extends into the grass meadow to offer an outdoor sitting area.

Left and opposite –
The silver grey of the timber cladding allows the house to sit discreetly among the trees, even during the winter months; the integrated garage and sheltered entrance porch are particularly advantageous during the cold weather.

Right and pages 114–19 – The key family living spaces are all at ground-floor level, within an easy and fluid open layout that includes the kitchen at one end, the dining area and the seating zone; the master suite is also on the ground floor.

'We have everything we need on one level, which works perfectly for us,' says the owner. 'We really built the house so that it would be possible for us to grow old there and actually we hardly ever go upstairs. But it's good for the children too. They are twelve and sixteen now and they each have their own bedroom and bathroom, and they share the television room. Sometimes it's almost impossible to get them down unless dinner is ready.'

On the ground floor, the plan evolved through careful consideration of practicality and functionality. Given the Norwegian weather, with its regular rainfall, Saunders decided to create a vast porch over the main entrance area to the rear of the villa that would help shelter family and friends whatever the conditions. The clients wanted garaging for two cars and a storage space, so Saunders wove these elements into the design in conjunction with the porch, integrating them into the overall shape and composition of the house. Such elements helped to influence the dynamic form of the building, as the design process stepped from inside to outside and back again.

'In Norway it can rain for three hundred days a year, so a big covered entrance and a huge porch like this is great,' says Saunders. 'We start with content and what the clients want, given that the house is based on their needs, so it's a bonus when we also end up with a beautiful form like this. It's about hopping back and forth as we solve problems and then we let it sit a while before we have another round of sculpting the form. You might have the form in the back of your mind, but it's not the main driving force.'

Beyond the porch, the entrance hall forms part of a neat line of service spaces running along the more enclosed rear elevation of the house, with the stairway to the upper level and the laundry room also sitting within this axis. The rest of the ground floor is essentially devoted to an open-plan living area, as well as to the enclosed master suite at the opposite end of the villa. Holding the kitchen, dining zone and sitting area, the 'great room' is partially double-height, while connecting with the glass façade facing the water. Double doorways in this façade slide back to connect with a large wooden deck that forms an outdoor living room and a hinterland between the villa and the hillside.

The master suite offers a welcoming private realm, with a spacious bathroom and walk-in wardrobe. The bed is positioned so that it faces the view of the water, while the distinctive shape of the mono-pitch roof offers a sheltered veranda just outside. It is a calming, considerate space that offers Saunders' clients a semi-secluded and partially self-contained retreat.

'The house turns its back to the wind from the north and follows the sun,' says Saunders. 'The living room and the master bedroom look south and the roof does give you this protective element around the bedroom. We are always being asked to do flat roofs, as for some reason people often associate new architecture here with flat rooflines, but we love the idea of a sloping roof coming down to a point like this, and the roof is actually achieving a lot of different things in terms of its shape and line.'

Saunders' clients were particularly pleased with the joinery and the level of detailing and craftsmanship achieved by carpenters Nilsen & Andersen, both inside and outside. The use of different woods and timber finishes, including Dinesen white spruce for the floors, white-painted spruce boards for the ceilings and pine for the cladding, creates a sense of cohesion but also offers subtle textural contrasts; the use of wood also improves the acoustics

of the house and reduces any sound reverberation. Yet, for the family, perhaps the greatest pleasure comes from the way that the house connects so vividly with its surroundings.

'When friends come in by boat they can see how well the house works with the terrain and say how fantastic it is,' says the villa's owner. 'My favourite space is the living room because you can just sit there and look at nature, the sea and the sky. I'm very happy that the entire wall there is glass and, for me, the height and the glass are what make the entire house. We are very happy with that.

'The summer is incredible, but with that big glass wall you experience every season, and every kind of weather makes a stronger impression. We can see the clouds coming in and know that it will be raining in half an hour. You get a lot of sky and it changes all the time. It's a very special feeling.'

WAYS OF
WORKING

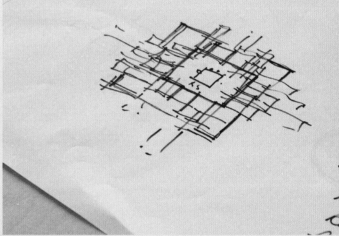

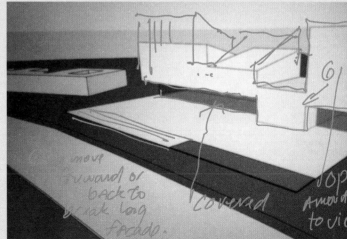

Overview

Given the sculptural character of so many of Todd Saunders' houses, cabins and studios, one might assume that his work is led primarily by a focus on form. In reality, this has never been the case for an architect who believes, above all, in the unique context of every project and responds accordingly. Saunders' buildings evolve through discussion and dialogue with his clients, as well as a detailed process of research, mapping and analysis exploring the specifics of a site, including its topography, the climate and the movement of the sun, the wind and the rain over time. The practice works from inside to outside and back again and it's only after developing a thoughtful response to a particular programme and setting that ideas begin to emerge about form.

'We have seen in the past that architects who start off with a strong form right away can get into trouble and that things soon begin to backfire,' says Saunders. 'So we always begin with content, based on the needs of the client. We list the rooms and spaces that are needed and we start making diagrams of these spaces as a way of beginning to organize them. Working diagrammatically helps to prioritize the different elements of the house and pare them down and gradually the form starts emerging from the programme, as we begin to hop back and forth from inside to outside. But it's always content-driven. It's based on the clients' needs because they don't start the process thinking about form and what the house is going to look like. So it's a real bonus for them when we do eventually come up with a form that is beautiful and distinctive.'

Clients – A Dialogue

One of the most valuable skills that Saunders has learned over the years is the ability to ask the right questions. The resulting dialogue between architect and client is an essential first step in the architectural design process and lays the foundation for a successful building. This thoughtful conversation is the basis for mutual understanding within a relationship that is both professional and personal at one and the same time. Often compared to a doctor-patient relationship, it is a meeting of minds that can be intense and even intimate, yet also therapeutic and rewarding. Such discussions, given their importance, may take place over the course of many months.

On a prosaic level, it's only by asking the right questions about the requirements and wishes of a client – and their family – that a meaningful and accurate programme can develop for a project. There's a whole category of questioning around practical and functional requirements, including the number of bedrooms or the need for dedicated spaces for work or relaxation. But then there's another collection of more poetic questions that ask about a client's dreams and ambitions for a building and how they see this house matching their lives. Thirdly, and just as importantly, there is a set of questions that seeks to establish how the project might be judged upon its completion or, in other words, what are the criteria for its success? How, for instance, will this building make people feel, or how will it be remembered, or what kind of an impact will it make upon its setting and surroundings?

'We have always spent a lot of time asking questions before we draw anything,' Saunders says. 'We really need to get to know the clients and understand what they want from a project, as well as what the site demands. It's only then that we can actually start to look at solving some problems and thinking about ideas, It's a long relationship that carries you through a project that might take two or three years to complete, so you have to devote some time to getting to know one another. For myself, I'd also like to know if they are willing to experiment and do something different to anything that we have done before? And it's good to think that we will learn something not just from the project but also from the client, because it is a collaborative process.

'We talk about what they love to do, what they might have loved or what challenged them about their previous house, and slowly, as you get to know them, they do begin to talk about their inner wishes and dreams. That's when it starts to get exciting. Once you establish some confidence and the clients begin to open up, then you start getting down to specific needs. Depending on how well the clients really know what they want, that dialogue might take a couple of months.'

There is also the important issue of commitment. Designing and building a house is a life-affirming decision, but one that demands a great deal of time, energy and creativity, as well as a healthy budget. The initial dialogue between architect and client explores this level of commitment, while establishing a positive spirit for a special kind of journey, or adventure, that will be positive and pleasurable.

Most of Saunders' clients clearly have a strong appreciation, from the very beginning, of what it is that they want to achieve, and know their own minds.

They are, for the most part, looking to build bespoke homes that will be 'forever houses', and already have a particular understanding of modern architecture. They tend to be entrepreneurial, creative and imaginative, while also open to original ideas and fresh thinking. Just as importantly, they share with Saunders a love of nature and an ingrained respect for the land.

Site – A Context

In most instances, clients come to Todd Saunders and his practice knowing that he will look after the landscape that they love. This has been the case in both Canada and Norway, including larger projects such as the Fogo Island Inn and sensitive rural developments such as Carraig Ridge in the foothills of the Rocky Mountains (see page 246), as well as numerous private homes. Many of Saunders' projects have been built in environmentally sensitive sites, where the lightest of touches upon the landscape is an essential requirement.

Clockwise from top left –
A running trail on Fogo Island, Newfoundland, Canada, where Saunders has designed a hotel, artists' studios and other projects; a collection of five hundred pertinent questions gathered over the course of a working year; a cladding study developed with the studio's in-house carpenter; site visits, which form a key part of the research and design process; the 'stilts' that hold up the cantilever of the Fogo Island Inn hotel.

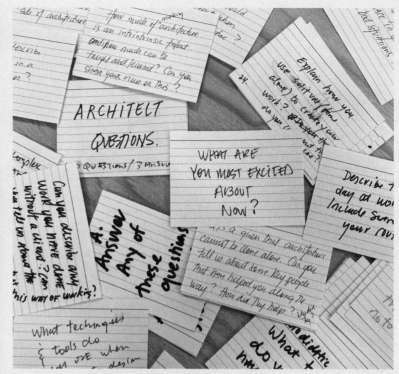

Clockwise from top left – The studio library, under construction in the first two images, offers opportunities for gathering books and reference works, but also samples of materials; a model of a public sculpture designed by the studio and made by the in-house carpenter; a view of the Bergen office and studio of Saunders Architecture, not far from the architect's own home, Villa S; the home library at Villa S; an early model of Villa Austevoll; and an early diagrammatic project drawing.

For residential clients such as the owners of Villa Austevoll (see page 18) or Villa Tyssøy (see page 156), the house sits within a setting that they have known and loved for many years, adding to the desire to preserve and conserve the natural beauty of the surroundings as far as possible. The practice's mapping of a site, which is done as part of an initial site survey, not only documents contours and sight lines, therefore, but also the trees, the vegetation, and any other natural features.

'Getting to know a site really well has almost been like a religion for me,' says Saunders. 'Digital surveys have made things easier for us, so we can get every pine tree down on the map as early as we can and start working with the land. It's like going with the grain of the wood, rather than struggling against it. I have been working with a surveyor in Norway for twenty years and he will get all the contours right, map all the trees, note any rock outcrops, and then we will build both a physical model and a digital model of the site. When the clients come in to see some ideas, we will put the proposed house onto that physical site model so that they have a full understanding of how it will sit in the landscape.

'But we are also looking at the path of the sun, the wind directions and the climatic conditions of the property. Norwegians and Canadians know where the sun comes up and goes down and they also know that these things matter. They appreciate the land and the pine trees and the rocks, because nature is such a powerful part of both cultures. I think that's why people come to us, because we celebrate the landscape.'

Inside-Outside

Saunders' houses always evolve from the inside out. They begin with a programme agreed with the client, encompassing their requirements and placed within the clear parameters of a working brief and a budget. Generally, Saunders' clients opt for a sociable and multi-faceted living space, or 'great room', combining the kitchen with spaces for dining and relaxation. This becomes the communal hub for family life, often sitting at the centre of the plan and focused upon a key vista. Service zones and storage tend to be pushed to the rear of such space, often sitting within spine walls, to avoid disturbing the overall sense of scale, proportion and volume.

Increasingly, Saunders' clients tend to opt for a degree of separation between children's bedrooms and a generously sized master suite, with the great room often sitting between them in single-storey houses. Annexes are an option for children or guests, as seen at Villa Tyssøy or Villa AT (see page 68), while clients might also need a dedicated work space, home office, music room or library (see Villa S, page 192, or Villa S+E, page 40). In some instances, requirements can be more specific or unusual, as with the request for a number of students flats on the lower level of Villa S+E. It's only by modelling such requirements from the outset that the practice can begin to establish initial ideas for the plan of a house.

'We will develop a room programme, including the number of rooms and the rough sizes of the spaces,' says Saunders. 'That's the diagrammatic and quantitative part of the process. And then we start to go backwards and forwards thinking about whether spaces need to be bigger or smaller, but also talking to the clients about what they want to see when they wake up in the morning, whether they want to be able to talk to other people when they are cooking in the kitchen or if they want it to be closed off. It's qualitative but we do spend plenty of time on it because we are refining what the clients want and that becomes the basis for the overall size of the house and the spaces within it. This helps to make each house as individual as the people who live in it.

'Only by doing the room programme can we say to the client, the house will be this particular size and it will cost this much to design and build. That's what we can take responsibility for and that's the information passed to the quantity surveyor so that there is accountability. We can work out a fixed budget based on the programme and size, but we also make clear to the clients that if they want to go for a more expensive kitchen or expensive fixtures and fittings then that's something that's up to them and it becomes additional spending. It's all set out very clearly, because the financial side can be quite frightening for some clients.'

Form

Once these room diagrams are more or less established, with a sense of how these various spaces should relate to one another, then Saunders and the practice can begin to explore ideas about the form of the house. This connects with research on site specifics, sight lines and climatic conditions, all of which are fully taken into account. Outdoor rooms and hybrid spaces that might be partially sheltered and open to the view become an important element within the overall outline of the building. Integrated verandas, balconies and porches act as part of the blurring process between inside and outside living, yet they are also designed with the movement of the sun and weather conditions in mind.

'We do go back and forth from form to plan, as the buildings become more sculptural and refined,' Saunders says. 'It's "functional sculpture" in a way, because the form is driven by the function, position and orientation of the spaces in and around the house. With houses to some extent you can work on plan, function and form simultaneously and hold these different elements in your mind at the same time, which makes it more dynamic and interesting, but you still land a good piece of architecture.'

Ideas – Proposals

Saunders describes the evolution of ideas for a project as essentially 'Darwinist'. While a dozen or more initial suggestions and proposals might be considered for a house, some begin to fall away within 'the survival of the fittest'. Eventually, two or three ideas might be developed further and presented to the client.

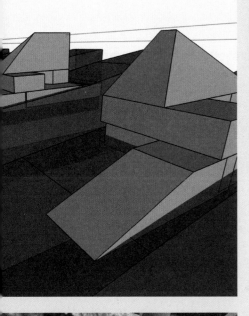

Top left – Initial model
studies for a new
visitor contact station
at Katahdin Woods
and Waters National
Monument in Maine,
United States.

Top right – A crab dinner
at the Shed, an award-
winning dining pavilion
alongside the Fogo Inn,
Newfoundland, Canada.

Middle row – Drawings,
models and prototypes,
all forming part of the
research and design
process.

Bottom row –
A 25-square-metre
(270-square-foot)
prototype building
being constructed at
the studio's workshop.

'Sometimes you might start with as many as twenty ideas for a project but you have to begin to navigate your way through them and have your client on board with the decision-making process. Decisions have to be made to move the creative process forwards, so if you have a client who is feeling unsure then it can come back at you. That's why it's important to understand one another and keep moving forwards as part of this Darwinist process.

'We might show the client three ideas and look at the pluses and minuses of each one and then it might become obvious what we like and what the client likes. But we do give it some time and there might be a pause of a week or two to really think about it. As architects, we might want to try and convince a client that a particular idea meets all their needs but, on the other hand, sometimes we might mix two ideas together to create something new. Slowly, slowly things start to fall into place and there is a moment when you start talking about very specific details, which means that the client has accepted the big idea. It's a really good feeling when you realize

that a client is comfortable with the big idea. That's an exciting moment.'

Collaboration

While the creative team in Saunders' Bergen office is relatively small, his projects are carried forwards by a much more extensive network of consultants, designers and artisans. As well as the surveyors and experts already touched upon, the practice will also draw in additional support, particularly when working abroad, where a local project architect will be added to the team. Having someone available on the ground in such circumstances means that the practice can keep a constant eye on the construction process and respond to any queries and questions from the builders and artisans on site, as they would at home in Norway.

Importantly, Saunders and the practice have always involved themselves intimately with the construction process and forged links with teams of artisans working on their projects in Scandinavia,

North America and other parts of the world. For Saunders himself, the practical building skills learned during his early years offer a valuable frame of reference, along with his own ongoing building projects at his country cabin.

The architect enjoys spending time in the workshop, not just developing architectural models but also working with trusted carpenters and joiners on prototypes. For the Aurland Lookout, for example, part of the structure was mocked up and brought into the office, while for Villa S and Villa Austevoll prototypes were made of the staircases. Similarly, for the Fogo Island Inn, one of the guest bedrooms was fully mocked up as a test case.

'I would say that we use more physical models than other practices but also more detail prototyping,' says Saunders. 'It might be the corner details of a house or a small building constructed in the workshop. We can directly commission the carpenters and reach a much higher level of craft through close collaboration.

It's another strand of our research, in a way, where we can develop ideas and concepts, while testing all the details, and those ideas inform our projects.'

Construction & Completion

Close communication continues through the construction process, with Saunders and his team spending a good deal of time on site. The practice takes a responsive approach to the build, refining and clarifying details for the construction team as needed. Even when working remotely, email, iPads and Zoom calls allow for continuing dialogue about finishes and fine-tuning.

'We try to get involved in the construction process more and more, especially towards the end to tie everything together. In our contracts we suggest a set of site meetings that are milestones, including the initial site visit with the builders and all the contractors involved. The design process can be relatively quick and playful, while the construction process tends to be slow, but I like it that way. I used to get impatient, but now I enjoy the fact that these things do take time and the best houses are the ones where we are there on site and getting involved.

'I grew up in a family of builders and as a child I helped build our lake cabin with my Dad and my uncles. Then Tommie Wilhelmsen and I built the cabin together that got us known, so I am constantly getting my hands dirty. When I constructed my own house, Villa S, the carpenters could see that perhaps I couldn't build something as well as they could, but they understood that I knew what I was doing. I really admire carpenters and artisans, and there are five or six that I could mention that have taught me more about construction than I have learned from my professors at architecture school.'

This love of craft and materiality carries through the design and build of Saunders' houses, with particular attention to detailing and surfaces. Yet, at the same time, Saunders is also happy to collaborate with interior designers and furniture designers on the finishing touches to a house. In this respect, as an architect he is atypically unpretentious and accepts the value that an interior designer can bring to a space in terms of character and personality.

A case in point is Villa S, Saunders' own house, where he worked on the interiors with artist and designer Hannes Wingate, looking at the choreography of the furnishings and furniture. Wingate also worked on the interiors of Villa AT, while Eero Koivisto collaborated on the interiors of Villa S+E, and Stine Homstvedt on Villa Refsnes (see page 138). In each case, these designers brought something fresh and original to the project, adding to the collaborative ethos that pervades Saunders' practice.

Clockwise from top left – A model of the staircase at Villa S; the boathouse under construction at Lily Pad, Ontario, Canada (see page 84); senior architect Ryan Jorgensen in Banff National Park, Alberta, Canada; Zoom meetings during the pandemic of 2020–21; meetings and conversations with design collaborators from the Swedish practice Claesson Koivisto Rune; in-house carpenter Uldis Rimsa; private house in progress, Barr'd Islands, Fogo Island; construction of a new prototype in the workshop.

WAYS OF WORKING

Clockwise from top left – Good times with Nancy Bendtsen from Inform Interiors in Vancouver, Canada; architect Ryan Jorgensen with Selkirk Mountains local Nicoline Beglinger; Sina Sangolt Saunders at the Fogo Island Inn in Newfoundland, Canada; Todd Saunders sanding the floors at his new home on Fogo Island; Lucas St. Clair from the client team at Katahdin Woods and Waters National Monument in Maine, United States; laying out this book with graphic designer Ian Holcroft; Todd Saunders with mentor Jane Durante, who encouraged him to become an architect.

Clients – Discipline & Pleasure

One of the elements that helps to set Saunders' work apart is the balance between discipline and rigour on the one hand, and an openness to collaboration and partnership on the other. Within architectural circles, where the concept of creative control seems to be a perpetual source of tension, this is something of a rarity in itself. Yet Saunders sees these working dialogues with artisans, technicians and designers from other disciplines as a way of enhancing his projects and his practice. Similarly, the architect's professional relationships with his clients offer opportunities for learning and growth just as much, if not more so, than the pursuit of academic or theoretical strands of thought.

This is true of Saunders' many house projects, but also of situations such as the Fogo Island Inn, or Carraig Ridge, where the client is not necessarily the end-user of the building. Here, too, there is a process of learning combined with what could be described as a warm spirit of engagement. It is worth noting that Saunders is one of the few architects to talk about architecture as something that should be a source of fun and enjoyment, as well as enhancement or betterment.

'Teaching gives us a theoretical perspective and the building research that we do helps to push the limits of theory, so we are testing ideas on ourselves and then bringing them into our paid projects,' says Saunders. 'But when it comes to houses, one of my criteria for working with people is the hope that I can contribute to their lives but also learn something from them. They are people who really know who they are and what they want to do in life, so they challenge me in a positive way.

'It's a real misconception that architects like me want carte blanche, because that's the worst thing. I want someone who is going to question me in an intelligent way and in return we try to make the design process a lot of fun for them. They are ready to take on this task of making a house, with all the work involved, and we want it to be a pleasurable and positive process. In most cases, this is the first and last house that they will build for themselves and so we all take it seriously, of course, because they might be living in the house for the rest of their lives. But they should also be able to enjoy that process because, like getting a custom-made suit or dress, it should be a real pleasure to create a tailored home for yourself and your family.'

HOUSES
— PART TWO

VILLA REFSNES

Starefossen, Bergen
Norway

One of the great pleasures of living in the picturesque port city of Bergen is the way that many of its urban neighbourhoods offer easy connections with the mountains and forests. This is especially true of desirable enclaves such as Starefossen, which sits upon one of the hillsides that overlook the centre of the city, the university district and the winding waterways that lead, eventually, out to the open sea. Houses here, such as Villa Refsnes, are blessed with some of the best views of 'the city between the seven mountains' yet are just a few minutes away from the walking and hiking trails that take you around the lake at Svartediket, or into the woodlands of Bergen's natural preserves or towards the famous peak of Ulriken.

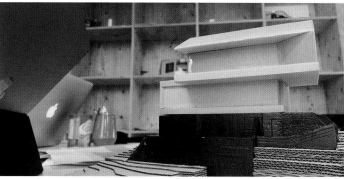

Opposite – The new villa replaced the uppermost section of the building inherited by Saunders' clients; the former residence had a very limited sense of connection with the views, which was fully rectified within the design of the modern two-storey structure, as seen here in the first study model.

Given the multiple advantages of living in Starefossen, it is no wonder that Bjørn Erik and Elisabeth Oroug Refsnes embraced the opportunity to settle here when they inherited a forties house that had once belonged to Bjørn's grandmother. The house sat within a well-sized garden, with a lower level built in stone and the upper storeys in timber. But, unfortunately, there was a limited sense of connection with the cityscape and very few windows facing the open view.

'The house has been in the family since it was new and my mother grew up here, with her two brothers,' says Bjørn Erik, a financial auditor. 'It is a great location but the layout of the house was very old-fashioned, with a small kitchen and small bedrooms and no windows upstairs that faced the city. So what kept growing in our minds was the idea of having something new and completely different.'

Initially the couple began looking into remodelling the existing house, but realized that it would prove a long, complicated and expensive process. Eventually, they recognized that it might be altogether simpler and more rewarding to replace the house with a building that was not only tailored to the views and to the setting, but also to the needs of a family with two children and their desire for more generously scaled living spaces.

'I had feelings for the old house, because I spent Christmas and 17 May [Norway's national day] here many times when I was a child,' says Bjørn Erik. 'But that's also why I felt that the site deserved a real project and that we could not just put up anything here. We really wanted a modern home, built for the way we use houses today. We wanted larger bedrooms, larger bathrooms and the opposite of the spaces that the old house already had.'

A mutual friend introduced the couple to Todd Saunders and a conversation began about designing and building the bespoke house that became Villa Refsnes. The site came with a number of sensitivities and restrictions related to the building's height and its relationship to neighbouring houses, but these challenges also acted as a spur to the creative process.

'It's really one of the best addresses in the city because it's like an amphitheatre with the city and the water below you and the mountains above you,' says Saunders. 'The view is amazing for everyone who lives here, so you do have to be careful to respect the neighbourhood and make the most of the setting and the western sunsets over the ocean. The first ideas we had were about flipping the plan of the old house and having the family's living space on the top floor and then the sleeping area below. We knew that we could do something better here.'

"This is what it's all about for me. It's cooking it down until you have something that's pure, and that's what we are doing here at Villa Refsnes.

— TODD SAUNDERS

Previous pages – From this perspective, the winding street pattern can be fully appreciated as it ascends the hillside, as well as the way that the villa occupies this garden setting, framed by the curving roadway.

Opposite and below – The villa is accessed from the rear of the house, which is relatively enclosed, ensuring privacy from the streetscape.

Following page – The dominant upper storey of the villa projects outwards to embrace the open view of the city while helping to provide shade and shelter for the bedroom level below.

Saunders and his clients decided to keep the stone plinth of the old house, which now holds a separate and self-contained apartment at basement level, while sweeping away the upper two storeys of the original structure. The plinth helps to anchor the house to the site, creating a neat base station for the new building above, with its steel framework and coat of crisply detailed white spruce.

The ground floor is devoted to the main entrance, accessed from the uppermost portion of the site, and to a central media and family room. Benefiting from an open vista, the master suite sits to one side of this centre point, while the children's bedrooms are placed to the other. This gentle sense of separation allows the two generations to enjoy some privacy within a flexible plan that gives the children their own dedicated part of the house.

Yet it's the upper storey that is purposefully dominant. Here, the south-east facing part of the house slides gently outwards over the sleeping zone below. This relatively simple but dynamic step not only energizes the outward form and appearance of the building but also unlocks the potential for balconies facing the city. Towards the front of the villa there is a semi-sheltered balcony, or elevated veranda, sitting within the outline of the building and protected by the overhang of the pitched roof. Yet the plan also

provides a roof deck on the north-western elevation, creating a choice of outdoor spaces, each one enjoying an open vista.

Inside, this part of the house is arranged as a 'great room': an open-plan living space orientated towards the bank of sliding glass that feeds out to the semi-protected balcony and frames the panorama of Bergen below. This is a warm, welcoming and finely crafted family space, with interiors designed in conjunction with Stine Homstvedt from SCH Interior Design, and cabinetmaker Georg Guntern of GG Möbel. Douglas fir floors help to unify this generously scaled space, with a custom kitchen and island at one end, a dining zone towards the middle, and a seating area at the other end. An elegant storage wall sits to the rear, holding a fireplace as well as storage and shelving made by Guntern. At the same time, this integrated monolith protects the staircase behind it and disguises a modest washroom. This arrangement allows the family to enjoy the luxury of open space, while leading everyone inevitably towards the light and the vista.

The detailing is crisply done and finely executed both within and without. It is a thoughtful process of reduction, or architectural editing, that amplifies the form and outline of the building externally, while providing calm and ordered living spaces internally.

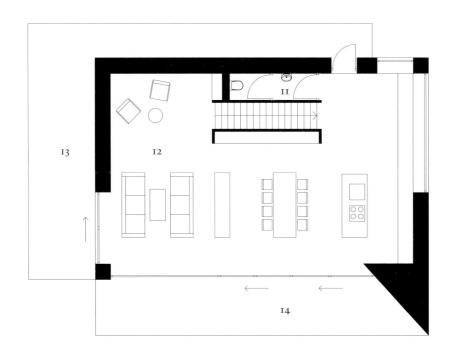

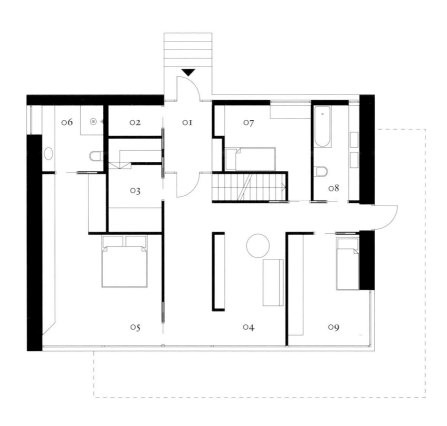

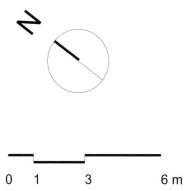

GROUND FLOOR

01 Entrance
02 Wardrobe
03 Storage
04 TV room
05 Master bedroom
06 Bathroom
07 Bedroom 1
08 Bathroom
09 Bedroom 2

1ST FLOOR

11 WC
12 Living room, dining room & kitchen
13 Balcony 1
14 Balcony 2

0 1   3   6 m

'It's all about paring it down to the essential elements,' says Saunders. 'This is what it's all about for me. It's cooking it down until you have something that's pure, and that's what we are doing here at Villa Refsnes. Everyone looks at it and says it's very simple and clean but that's part of the design process. Like Churchill said, "Sorry for the long letter but I didn't have time to write a short one." We write shorter sentences because we are thinking about how we can get the most out of the house and a limited area. In that respect, Villa Refsnes has been very successful.'

For Bjørn Erik and Elisabeth Oroug Refsnes, the decision to commission a new house gave them not only the opportunity for a fresh beginning, but the chance to create a home that truly reflected the needs of the family: 'It has exceeded all of my expectations,' says Elisabeth, who works as a group controller. 'The feeling of living in the house

is amazing, especially compared to what I first imagined when we started thinking about the project. I love everything about it but the upstairs room is my favourite. We spend most of our time here: the kids do their homework here, we make dinner here, and it's where we all gather together.'

For Bjørn Erik, any worries about replacing a building that meant so much to him and to his mother have been swept away by the new house. His mother and his uncles have all embraced the design. 'My mother came to see the house while we were building it and she cried,' he says. 'I think it was ninety-nine per cent happy tears and one per cent for the old house. Now she's here at the house quite often and sometimes we don't even talk that much, because she sits here and enjoys the view and the weather. There will always be feelings connected to something like this, but she really likes it here now.'

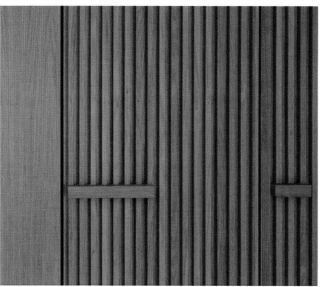

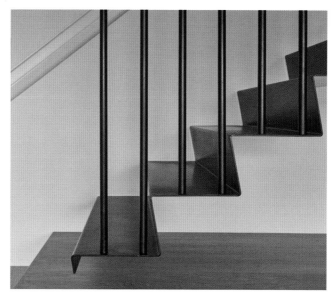

Previous pages – The upper storey is largely arranged as one open-plan, multi-purpose living space with the kitchen at one end, a dining area to the centre and then a seating zone; the elevated and sheltered veranda alongside can be used as a natural extension of this living space.

Left and opposite – Integrated storage throughout helps to simplify the interiors and maximize the sense of space. The bespoke unit with its bookshelves and drawers, sitting next to the integrated fireplace, helps to shelter the stairwell, which is positioned behind it.

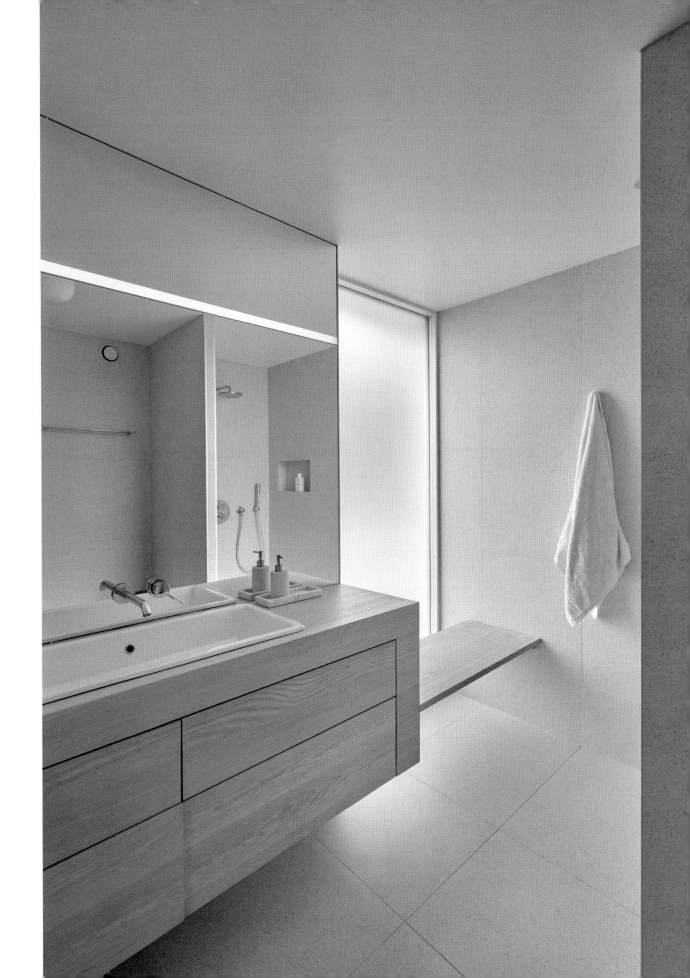

Previous pages – The interiors were designed in conjunction with Stine Homstvedt and cabinetmaker Georg Guntern, who worked on much of the fitted furniture and storage, including the combined storage unit and desk in the bedroom.

Left – Protected by the overhanging roofline, the balcony becomes an outdoor room, offering a bird's-eye view out across the city and towards the harbour.

VILLA TYSSØY

Tyssøy, Bergen
Norway

Like a sculpture or a piece of land art, Villa Tyssøy is a characterful composition that can be appreciated from all directions. Given the natural beauty of its island setting, it was particularly important to both Todd Saunders and his clients that the house should not only be a gentle presence in the landscape but that it should also have a sculptural quality. Consisting of three distinct elements framed by a low stone wall, the house can be fully valued from any direction, with no secondary elevation or aspect of afterthought to this modern but modest farmstead.

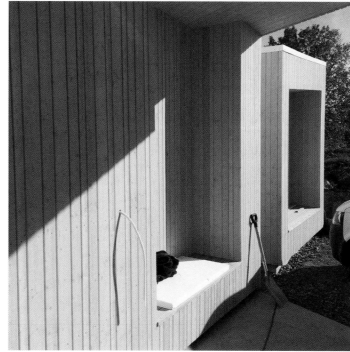

'We spent a lot of time looking at how we would place the house on the site and at how we would group these three small buildings together,' says Saunders. 'Keeping it low was another priority because it is situated on a ridge and if we had built too high then it would start to dominate. With a lot of our houses, like Villa Tyssøy, it is important that each side of the building has its own personality so you have a piece of architecture with a life of its own and a form that you can relate to no matter which direction you approach it from. The house stands alone, by itself, and it has to know what it is and who it is.'

The house was commissioned by Gerd Johanne Larsen and Hogne Tyssøy, who know this island setting intimately. Hogne Tyssøy's family have lived on the island, also known as Tyssøy, for six generations or more, and a number of his siblings and other relatives still have homes nearby. A parcel of land was passed down to Tyssøy, who works in the field of equities and investments, and he decided to build a new home in a place that he has known all of his life.

'My family bought a small farm here two hundred years ago and took the name of the island, which was quite normal in Norway at that time,' says Tyssøy. 'So we are island people and typically, back then, you might have a small farm but also work as a fisherman or in some kind of handcraft. About twenty years ago the island was connected to the neighbouring island with a bridge, and from that island there is an underwater tunnel to the mainland, so we are now only thirty minutes' drive from the centre of the city. It has become very easy to live here on the islands but still work in Bergen.'

The accessibility of the city, where both Larsen and Tyssøy usually work, added another layer of temptation to the idea of giving up the former family home in Bergen and relocating to the island full-time. The decision meant that the family could also indulge their love of the water, including commuting by boat to Larsen's family summer house around one hundred nautical miles to the north at Sognefjord. The couple wanted to build a 'forever house' at Tyssøy, but also felt a special sense of responsibility for a landscape that meant so much to them, and the need for a sensitive approach to these surroundings was one of the key factors that led them to Saunders and his practice.

'We are both interested in modern design, but it was really my wife, who is a teacher and very interested in architecture and art, who discovered Todd's work,' Tyssøy says. 'She had seen some of his earlier work and liked his approach very much, with its use of curved corners and its respect for the landscape, among other things, and so we met and there was a very good chemistry from day one. From studying some of Todd's projects we could see how he had a very good hand in respecting the surroundings and trying to create something that would fit with the landscape.

Previous pages – The house sits in a prominent position on the brow of a hill, offering a prime vantage point for appreciating the vista; at the same time neither architect nor client wanted the house to dominate, leading to a low building tied to the landscape.

Opposite – Dialogue and modelling led to the idea of three separate and interrelated structures, forming a modest modern farmstead, or 'tun', which sits well within this rural context; stone retaining walls form a low boundary, while bonding the building to the rocky topography.

"The house stands alone,
by itself, and it has to know
what it is and who it is.

— TODD SAUNDERS

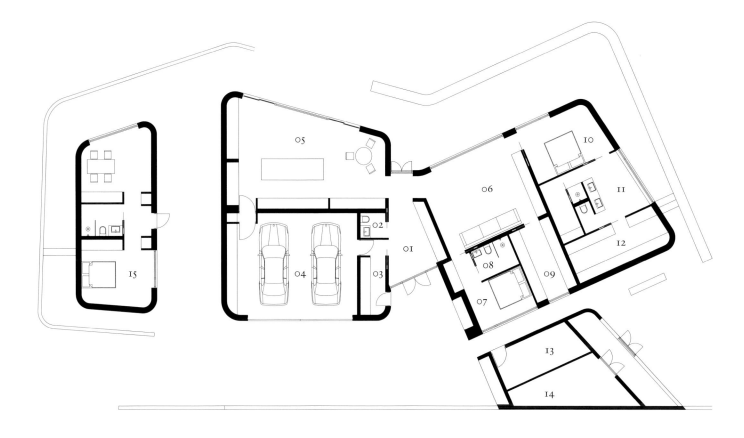

GROUND FLOOR

01 Entrance
02 WC
03 Laundry
04 Garage
05 Kitchen
06 Living room
07 Bedroom
08 Bathroom
09 Office
10 Master bedroom
11 Bathroom
12 Walk-in wardrobe
13 Storage
14 Storage
15 Annexe

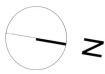

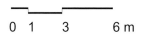
0 1 3 6 m

'The house is more or less like a sculpture, which we like very much, but we are on a small hill that is about thirty metres above sea level so in the end we actually lowered the building by about a metre, just to make sure that it was settled in the landscape. We saw that Todd has a very good understanding for these things.'

The programme for the house also began to evolve, but within a loose brief that enabled a good deal of creative freedom. The couple wanted a relatively small home, including a generously scaled master suite plus one guest bedroom. They also wanted to provide a semi-separate space for their son, who was just about to head off to university in Trondheim, and has since graduated and moved to Oslo. This led to the idea of an annexe, or satellite building, that was largely self-contained and has its own bathroom, kitchenette and living area as well as a bedroom. In addition to this studio, the family also wanted a neat storage structure that would offer both sealed and ventilated store spaces for multiple uses.

This led, eventually, to the idea of three small but complementary single-storey structures that together create a micro-compound or farmstead – or 'tun' as the Norwegians call it. Breaking the programme down into these components also helps in reducing the impact of the house upon its surroundings. At the same time, the weather conditions were another key factor taken into account, with the direction of the wind and climatic extremes influencing the final positioning and orientation of the residence.

The master building in the triptych is, in itself, composed of two conjoined wings with an entrance hallway at the meeting point, while the arrangements of the various spaces within these wings relates to key sight lines and vistas, including the waters of the fjord. One wing holds a garage, hidden away within the outline of the building, and then a combined kitchen and dining area with a bank of glass framing the open view. The other wing holds the sitting room and library, a guest room and a shared study, which both Larsen and Tyssøy use on a regular basis. The master suite sits at the far end of the house, beyond the sitting room, and consists of a bedroom, a large bathroom with an integrated sauna and also a walk-in wardrobe space and dressing room. This assembly of spaces creates an inviting private realm, set apart from both the guest accommodation and the annexe.

Pages 160–62 – The round edges of the timber-clad building soften the outline of the house, but also help to create a sculptural form sitting in an open landscape. The formation of the building also allows for terraces and outdoor spaces at key points around the villa.

Right – As well as responding to the topography and weather patterns, the design of the house relates to the mesmerizing views out across the water and neighbouring islands and islets, as seen here in the master bathroom, where the tub is thoughtfully positioned by the picture window.

'We are both very pleased with how things are,' says Tyssøy. 'It is very practical and everything is on one level, so it's very easy to move around. It is a very efficient house so hopefully we can live here for a long time, even as we grow older. We were pleased with the outcomes from a practical standpoint but also as a piece of art. In Norway there is a saying that you need to build at least three houses before you are satisfied, but we really think of this as our house for life.'

Saunders agrees that the tripartite house manages to combine both functionality and beauty. The evolution of the plan was especially rewarding, given the way that it enables easy, informal pattern of daily living while also opening up the key spaces to the landscape itself. Equally, the ideal of a 21st-century farmhouse that respects its island setting has particular resonance, while the white timber coat helps to add another layer of character and interest.

'In Norway, white houses are associated with the nicer farmhouses,' says Saunders. 'If it's red then it's usually a barn or a farmworker's house, but the white house is where the family lives and they are a sign that you have got yourself together and achieved something. With Villa Tyssøy the white cladding is really beautiful, because you can really see the shadows and the form as the light changes.

'It's a very clear project and it is like a piece of land art. But all these little moves came from studying the site and the family's own understanding of the setting. We knew where the best views would be and that the wind would often be coming from the north, so we were able to twist and turn accordingly. The garden is also low maintenance, with this simple, natural-stone wall, and then you have this grouping of the three buildings, which help each other. These elements are like a family of three in themselves.'

Left – The design of this modern farmstead encompasses three separate elements, designed with the same language and communicating closely with one another; this structure is devoted to storage, including this ventilated section, which can serve as a wood store.

Following pages – Seen from this perspective, the relationship between the storage structure and the main body of the house becomes clearer; the triptych of interrelated buildings also includes a self-contained annex used by the owner's grown-up son and visiting guests.

VILLA
GRIEG

Paradis, Lake Nordås
Bergen, Norway

The setting for Villa Grieg could hardly be more seductive or enticing. The house sits upon the brow of a hill, overlooking the waters of Lake Nordås and its collection of small islands. Situated around fifteen minutes' drive to the south of the city of Bergen, the neighbourhood has a semi-rural and almost bucolic quality, which comes partly from the wealth of woods and trees, but also from the open views of a unique and picturesque landscape where hills and coastal inlets combine.

The design of the house itself, for Alexander and Tonje Grieg, makes the most of this engaging, open vista. Todd Saunders describes the house as a kind of 'view finder', with the main living spaces looking out across water, while the side elevations are more protected and relatively enclosed, helping to sharpen the focus upon Lake Nordås itself. No wonder, perhaps, that the neighbourhood is known as 'Paradis'.

Alexander Grieg and his family have a long-standing connection with the area, stretching back to the 1880s, when Grieg's great-great-great-grandfather's cousin, the composer Edvard Grieg, commissioned the architect Schak Bull to design a summer house here for himself and his wife, soprano Nina Hagerup. Fusing references from Swiss chalets and Long Island beach houses, as well as Nordic vernacular, the house was christened 'Troldhaugen', or 'Troll Hill'. Now open to the public, Troldhaugen sits next to the shore and just down the hill from Villa Grieg.

There is a pleasing synergy in the fact that the new house designed by Saunders was also commissioned by a musician and his family. Grieg wanted to build a unique home for himself, his wife and teenage daughter, while also including an integrated recording studio. As such, the project is a live-work space with a subtle sense of separation between these two different realms.

'The most important elements of the project for me were having a place to work, namely the studio, but also making sure that the house should not interfere with the natural surroundings,' says Grieg. 'I would say that the house has actually made a big and positive difference to my life and also to my creativity.'

From the beginning, Grieg was determined to build a truly contemporary and dynamic 21st-century house. A long admirer of modern architecture, he began researching suitable architects for the project and, having noted the practice's work, was delighted to find that Saunders Architecture is based in Bergen.

'We began with a list of the things that we wanted from the house, but that list grew shorter and shorter as we began to understand what our needs as a family really are,' Grieg says. 'There was good chemistry from the start and Todd and I talked so much together about my likes and dislikes and what is important to me. We both took some time to go back and forth because the house was always about the long term.'

Previous pages – Coated in Kebony timber and bordered by mature pines, Villa Grieg rises and rotates, with the main body of the house floating above the ground plane, like a sculpted treehouse.

Opposite – The form of the steel-framed villa evolved through careful consideration of the site itself and the open views, including to Edvard Grieg's house below, with the idea that the house should never block the vista of Lake Nordås, but frame it instead.

Following pages – Seen from above, the central courtyard is clearly visible along with the solar array positioned on the roof of the house; shadows dance on the villa wall.

"I would say that the house has actually made a big difference to my life and also to my creativity.

— ALEXANDER GRIEG

There was a mutual understanding between architect and client, based on the realization that Villa Grieg is a 'forever house' and that time was a valuable tool for both in achieving the best possible outcome for the project. Saunders had just finished working on his own house, Villa S (see page 192), where he had begun experimenting with a number of ideas and design solutions that fed into the design process for Villa Grieg. These included the idea of elevating the main family spaces to enhance connections with the view, a fluid and open-plan living area, and a useful sense of separation between these more 'communal' parts of the house and spaces devoted to work or study.

'Villa Grieg followed on just after my house and they are around fifteen minutes' walk from one another, so Alex would come over a few times a week and see Villa S being constructed,' says Saunders. 'In a way, Alex's project could be seen as an evolution of some of the thinking behind my own home. But, at the same time, I think it's a better project in many ways because we were getting smarter all the time.'

As well as the pared-down programme for the house and studio requested by the Griegs, the other great driver for the project was, of course, the site itself. On the one hand, there was a need to protect the existing setting and the trees already in residence upon the hillside, while on the other there was the need to orientate the most important spaces in the house towards the open views of Lake Nordås.

'It's one of the best locations in Bergen to build a house,' Saunders says. 'So what we wanted to do was lift the building, so that you can see under the house towards the lake. So as you walk by, it doesn't create a wall to the landscape and instead you can see right through it.'

The only space on the ground floor of the villa, apart from a store room, is the music studio, which is set within a sculptural, sloping form that also holds the main entrance and the staircase. The stairs ascend this slope as they rise up towards the main living area and a long, horizontal band of glass framing a vista of the open landscape, which makes a striking impact as one steps into the private realm of the home. All of the family spaces, including two bedrooms, sit within this elevated part of the house, which floats above the ground plane on a series of pilotis.

HOUSES — PART TWO — VILLA GRIEG

Previous pages – The sloping element of the house holds Alexander Grieg's music studio but also the main entrance to the house and the staircase, which rises towards the light and the open vista.

Right – A view of the western elevation suggests how the design of the house adapts to the natural topography of the site, while the main living spaces on the principal level benefit from open views across the water, as well as flowing out to an integrated terrace and balcony.

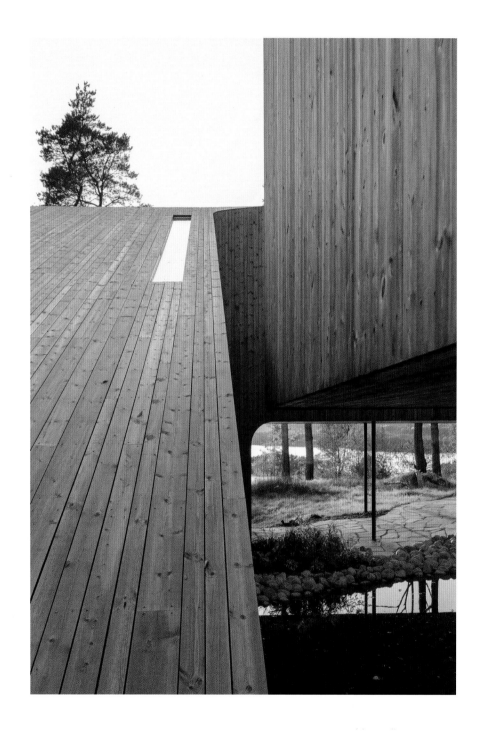

Left and opposite – The dynamism of the house is rooted in the journey it offers upwards to the principal storey and then around the enfilade of elevated spaces. At the same time, the villa is a modest presence in the wooded landscape, with the slender pilotis gently echoing the tree trunks.

HOUSES — PART TWO — VILLA GRIEG

A key point of difference between Villa Grieg and the more linear form of Villa S is the way in which this elevated portion of the building then wraps around a central void, an open courtyard with a pond at its centre. An enfilade of spaces and rooms looks inwards and across this lightwell, as well as outwards to the wider surroundings. In this respect, the form of the house could be compared to Lina Bo Bardi's exemplary Modernist icon Casa de Vidro (1950) in São Paulo, Brazil, which also features a collection of elevated rooms arranged around a central, double-height courtyard or atrium.

'I suspect that if I hadn't done my own house, then we might not have got Alex to sign off on the idea of lifting the house into the air,' says Saunders. 'But then we also used Kebony timber for the cladding, as we did at the Labrador museum [Illusuak Cultural Centre], and curving forms and curved glass rather like Villa AT (see page 68). So these things are all part of a constant learning process and a gradual metamorphosis of our thinking. Old ideas might fall away while curiosity pushes us to explore new ideas and experiment, which helps the work to evolve.'

The enfilade of spaces begins with an open-plan living space that combines the kitchen, dining area and family seating zone, arranged alongside a wall of floor-to-ceiling glass that slides back to form an open balcony facing the lake view to the west. Beyond this, on the north-western corner, there is a semi-sheltered veranda that sits within the outline of the building. Following the sequence of remaining spaces as they wrap around the open courtyard, there is a bedroom for the Griegs' daughter plus a bathroom and guest bedroom. Beyond this, a television room on the north-eastern corner forms a natural buffer zone that helps protect the most private element of the house holding the spacious master suite, which includes not only a generous bedroom but also the master bathroom and a walk-in wardrobe.

The overall footprint of the house is intentionally and purposefully modest. Any impact upon the natural character of the site has been carefully minimized, with very little in the way of artificial landscaping, as well as the sensitive preservation of the existing trees and vegetation. Rather than any grading of the site, the steel-framed building adapts to the undulations of the existing topography and the character of the hillside itself.

Yet the design of the building clearly maximizes the sense of connection with the landscape, creating a kind of observatory or belvedere that makes the most of the hillside context. In this respect, Villa Grieg might be compared to Todd Saunders and Tommie Wilhelmsen's Aurland Lookout, a 'skywalk' that was specifically created to facilitate a more direct relationship with a dramatic fjord and mountain setting on the western coast of Norway.

Left and opposite –
The house wraps around a central courtyard, and floats above the reflecting pond at its heart. This garden courtyard achieves many things, enabling an important degree of transparency that continues to allow a view of the lake through and under the house, while also introducing light and a sense of openness to all parts of the building.

Pages 186–89 –
The floor-to-ceiling windows turn the main living spaces into an elegant belvedere, with a long ribbon of glass looking over Lake Nordås. This open space includes the kitchen at one end, the dining area and then the seating zone, which connects with the adjoining balcony while also leading the way to the bedrooms and the private realm of the house.

Pages 190–91 –
Villa Grieg is best appreciated against the backdrop of its beautiful forest site.

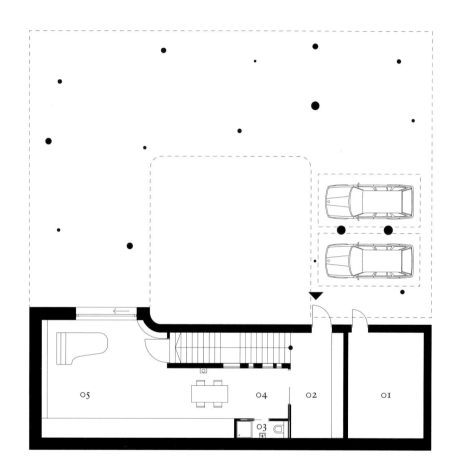

GROUND FLOOR

01 Storage
02 Entrance
03 Bathroom
04 Lounge & kitchen
05 Studio

1ST FLOOR

11 Entrance
12 WC
13 Laundry
14 Kitchen
15 Living room
16 Balcony
17 Bedroom 1
18 Bathroom
19 Bedroom 2
20 TV room & office
21 Bedroom 3
22 Walk-in wardrobe
23 Bathroom

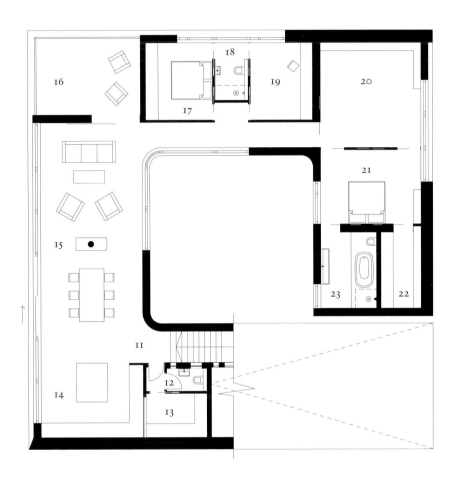

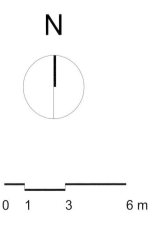

N

0   1   3   6 m

There's also a link to be made with Saunders' design of the Fogo Island Inn, on the Newfoundland island of the same name, which explores the idea of an elevated, stilted building to create a kind of platform that offers a more direct link with the surrounding land and sea.

'I'm often asked what influences I take from Scandinavia back to Canada, but no one asks me about the ways in which I might translate ideas from Canada to Norway,' says Saunders. 'Some aspects of Canadian architecture, such as the idea of lifting fishermen's huts and other buildings by the sea, have helped me create better buildings here. The Fogo Island Inn uses the idea of a building raised up above the ground on legs, partly out of respect for the site. In five hundred years, when these buildings are gone, things will be almost the same as they were before rather than ruining the land, so having a softer touch on the landscape is part of the reason for taking that approach. Maybe this is where Norway gets a touch of Newfoundland architecture, in a way.'

For Saunders' clients, the new house is a delight: 'I am very proud of it,' says Grieg. 'I have a few favourite places in the house. There's a meditation spot upstairs next to the fireplace and grand piano. Sometimes I wake up really early, maybe five in the morning, and then I get up, make some coffee and sit in that spot. I meditate and almost disappear for a moment. It is almost transcendental. I love the break of dawn, which is completely quiet. Nothing happens, or maybe a fish jumps in the lake. It's very calm and the way that the view is framed is perfect. It is very good for my soul.'

VILLA
S

Tveiterås, Bergen
Norway

For any truly creative and imaginative architect, their own house offers a golden opportunity for experimentation and innovation. This was very much the case with Todd Saunders' Villa S, which was the first house that the architect built for his own family from the ground up. Multiple ideas and principles explored within the design of Villa S have influenced, in one way or another, many of the commissioned projects that have followed on. And, of course, the house has great importance and resonance on a personal level as the foundation stone of daily living for Saunders and his children.

'The house has given me a framework for my life and has really been a kind of refuge for me over the last few years,' says Saunders. 'It's so important to come home to a place where you can be by your hearth and lay your head down, but that also fits in with all of your needs. That's what this house has done and it has made my life a lot easier in a very practical sense. It has given so much more than I ever expected and become a place to create memories. It keeps on giving back to me.'

The location and setting of Villa S are certainly ideal for Saunders. The house sits around fifteen minutes' drive south of Bergen, within a semi-rural enclave that is a walk away from the architect's studio and office, while a number of clients and friends also live close by. The site itself was once a small communal park in the garden city of Tveiterås, which was laid out in the thirties by the celebrated Norwegian architect Leif Grung. A pioneering Modernist, Grung designed thirty-six houses here, including one for himself.

'It used to be a farm and Leif Grung got together with the owners and developed a plan for a garden-city neighbourhood, with around seventy houses,' says Saunders. 'He was educated in Stockholm and then came back to Norway and was known as the Frank Lloyd Wright of Bergen between the wars. He was quite well known and wore a big hat and drove a nice car. He was certainly an interesting personality and his son, Geir Grung, also became a celebrated architect, based in Oslo.'

Falsely accused of collaboration at the time of the Nazi occupation of Norway during World War Two, Grung committed suicide in 1945, falling to his death from a cliff close by. A few years after his death, he was honoured with Norway's most important architectural prize, the Houen Foundation Award, having left behind an influential legacy of houses and buildings, many of which fused a deep-rooted respect for Modernism with a love of landscape. This was very much the case at Tveiterås.

'I can see many of Grung's houses from Villa S,' Saunders says. 'They are all facing west and perched really nicely on the site. I lived in one of his houses for a year while I was building my own and experienced this thirties version of modern architecture, then tried to create my own eighty years later. One of the big differences was that the kitchens in Grung's houses were really small, but the kitchen at Villa S is part of one of the biggest spaces in the house.'

Previous pages – The new house sits in a semi-rural setting, within the garden city of Tveiterås, laid out by the Modernist architect Leif Grung; mature trees climbing the slope of the gentle hillside behind the house form a verdant backdrop.

Opposite – The design process was informed not only by the site itself but by the weather patterns, with Saunders intent on creating sheltered spaces and outdoor rooms that could be used by the architect and his children all year round. The top-left image shows Saunders with a chainsaw on day one.

"The house has given me a framework for my life and has been a kind of refuge for me over the last few years.

— TODD SAUNDERS

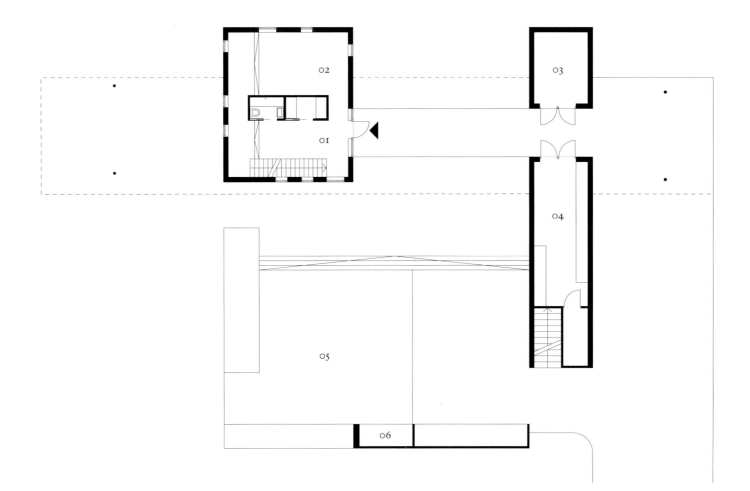

GROUND FLOOR

01 Entrance
02 TV room
03 Storage
04 Storage
05 Outdoor area
06 Firewood

1ST FLOOR

11 Balcony 1
12 Living room
13 Bedroom 1
14 Bedroom 2
15 Bathroom
16 Laundry
17 Kitchen
18 Balcony 2
19 Master bedroom
20 Walk-in wardrobe & bathroom

2ND FLOOR

21 Outdoor area
22 Library
23 Bookshelf
24 Outdoor area
25 Roof

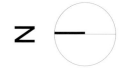

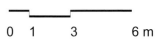

0   1   3   6 m

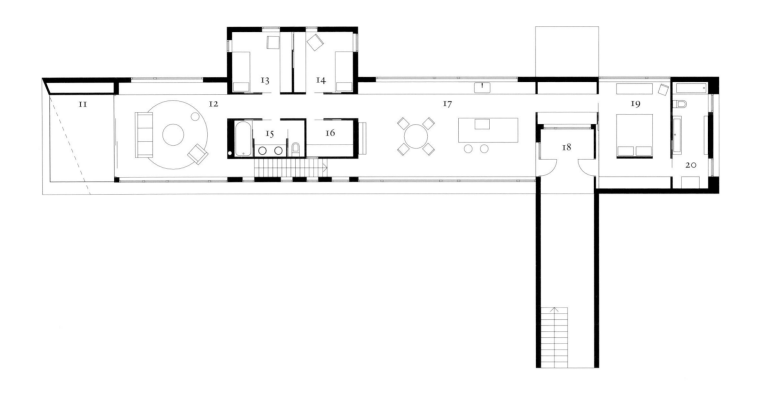

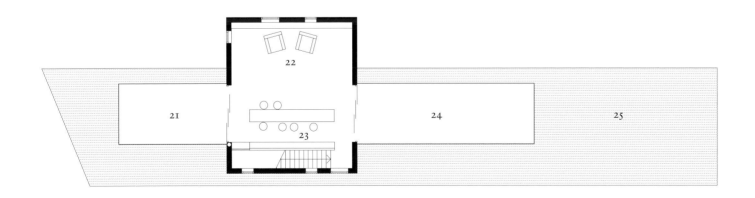

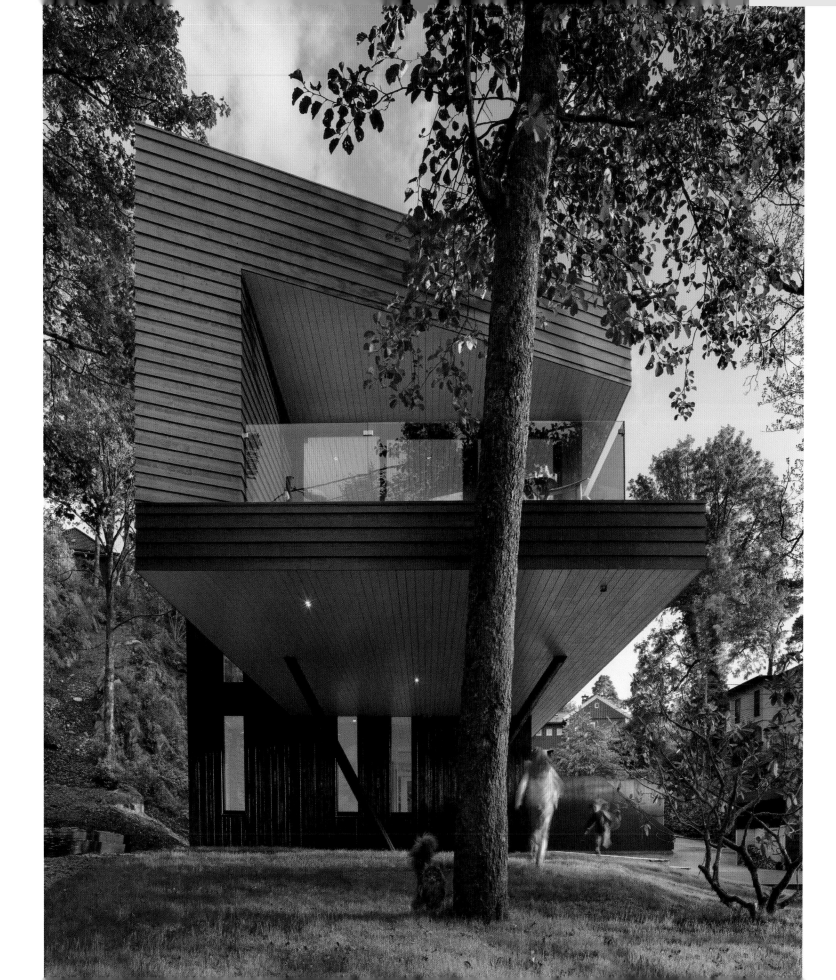

HOUSES — PART TWO — VILLA S

Pages 196–201 – The decision to elevate the main living spaces allowed Saunders to create a semi-protected entry sequence, terrace and play area under the house, which can be used whatever the weather; additional decks and terraces are also situated on the principal storey and on the roof.

Left – The sequence of arrival from the car port through to the entrance hall is sheltered, with the hallway itself offering a calm and welcoming space, which also includes integrated coat cupboards and storage, as well as a daybed for making the process of taking shoes off and on much easier.

The design of Villa S evolved not only in response to the needs of Saunders and his family, but also to the nature of the site and, in particular, the weather. It can rain in Bergen for as many as 250 days in a year, serving as a brake on outside living, which was a source of frustration for Saunders. He began thinking about designing a home that would offer sheltered exterior space as well as protected interiors.

'I decided to lift the house off the ground, so that almost the entire building becomes an umbrella for the outside spaces beneath it. So, when they were younger, my daughters could go outside and use the swings under the house even when it was raining. There was no excuse not to go outside and play and, for me, I can go and fix my bike or set up my camping gear and not worry about the rain. The whole house became a kind of tent sheltering these fresh-air spaces.'

This was another key point of difference with Grung's houses, which have a very limited provision of indoor-outdoor spaces such as porches and verandas. Saunders also decided to stretch the house out lengthwise on the site, maximizing both the connections with the gardens and the views, but also creating a more substantial undercroft. The main body of the steel-framed, spruce-clad house is lifted up by slim structural pillars, and also by the clean line of storage units near the integrated carport at one end of the house, and by the dedicated entrance unit further along. This 'promenade architecturale' creates a heightened sense of anticipation on the short journey to the front door, sheltered from the elements by the building above.

The entry sequence itself combines practicality with a sense of arrival. The hallway is spacious and inviting, with a suspended sculptural staircase to one side made of plywood with a coating of fibreglass. Coat cupboards and a rest room sit to one side, while a family den is hidden beyond in an outrigger at the rear of the building. The light and white palette of colours and materials within the hall sets up an ongoing contrast between these light surfaces and the black stain used on the timber cladding on the outside of the building, which allows the house to recede into the backdrop of trees and vegetation.

Moving upwards, the principal level of the house benefits from elevation in the way that the building both connects with the treeline and overlooks the front garden, while also enjoying the quality of the natural light. All of the principal living spaces and family bedrooms are arranged on this one level, with a spacious kitchen and dining area right at the centre of the floor plan. A service core holding the laundry room and a bathroom forms a pivotal point, or junction, providing a gentle degree of separation between the kitchen and the sitting room at the far end of the house, which – in turn – leads out onto a substantial sheltered balcony. Two modest children's bedrooms also sit next to the junction, located above the television room below. The master suite is at the opposite end of the house and is composed of a spacious bedroom, bathroom and a dressing room, which acts as a kind of buffer zone between this part of the house and the communal family living spaces.

Integrated storage units, window seats and other fitted elements simplify the spaces and help preserve a sense of clarity throughout. They also reduce the need for loose, free-standing furniture, yet Saunders still took the opportunity to collaborate on the design of the interiors for Villa S with Hannes Wingate, a Swedish artist and designer now based in America. Together, Saunders and Wingate worked on the choreography of the interiors and furnishings, adding another layer of texture and character, as well as modest splashes of colour that stand out against the prevailing palette of light and natural tones. It was a way of working that Saunders found both useful and uplifting.

'It was very collaborative, with Hannes focused on the furniture and textiles,' says Saunders. 'If we turned the house upside down, then anything that fell out would have involved Hannes. We also worked on Villa AT together (see page 68), and I have collaborated with other designers on the interiors of my projects. It doesn't always work having someone else involved, if there is no depth, but with Hannes and Eero Koivisto and others it's clear that they have a real love for what they do and there is this feeling that they are on your side and adding something to the project.'

(see page 68)

Right – The family kitchen and dining area sits at the centre of the house, also serving as a circulation point to the spaces to either end and a belvedere looking out onto the landscape.

Traditional ideas have also been reinterpreted and updated. In the sitting room, for example, the hearth remains an important focal point but the fireplace is set into one wall of the central service core. The library is another significant element, expressed at Villa S in the form of a library/study sitting on a modest upper level at the top of the building. This is a unique space, almost like a treehouse, which offers a particular sense of calm and quiet, helped by the way that the room sits both above and apart from the rest of the house. Rather like the idea of situating a generously proportioned master suite apart from children's or guest bedrooms, this principle of creating a sense of separation between a study space and the rest of the home is one that Saunders has applied to other residential projects for his clients.

'With my clients I have noticed that they work hard, and when it comes to the design of their home they like to have something that is a gift to themselves. That is often a nice bedroom, or a special bathroom, but for me the library is really my gift to myself. Books are really a part of me and I'm not that interested in television, so the library was a space somewhere between a want and a need.'

In this respect and many others, Villa S serves as a kind of laboratory of ideas. Yet at the same time the house offers a clear, almost graphic composition and a very ordered layout, with much of daily family living arranged upon one principal level. This translates into a very ordered, practical, functional house, as well as a home that is welcoming, layered and characterful.

'The house has really fulfilled my needs, as well as the dream of building my own home. It has given me much more confidence in what I do and I'd actually like to do a couple more over my lifetime. This won't be my last house for myself, I can guarantee that.'

Left – Saunders worked on the interiors in conjunction with Swedish designer and artist Hannes Wingate; modest bursts of colour stand out against the neutral tones of the walls and floors, while the furniture mixes contemporary designs with mid-century classics.

Opposite – The service core holding the bathroom and laundry within also plays host to an integrated fireplace, which forms a focal point in the sitting room; here the storage wall morphs into a window seat.

HOUSES — PART TWO — VILLA S

Previous pages –
The library sits at the top of the house, offering a quiet and contemplative space, removed from other aspects of daily living; a vintage workshop table serves as a desk while the room also plays host to books and art, including a framed photograph, *St George's Church in Lalibela, Ethiopia*, by Iwan Baan.

Left and opposite –
The master suite sits at the far end of the principal storey, with a dedicated bathroom and dressing area to either side; the room also connects with a secondary balcony, which – in turn – connects with the garden via a secondary hidden staircase.

Left and right – The garden and its outdoor rooms are an integral part of the house, rather than something distinct or separate; there is a choice of decks and terraces that frame family pleasures of all kinds for all four seasons.

Following pages – The interplay of light and dark space comes alive on a snowy night.

VILLA
R

Bømlo
Vestland, Norway

The decision to build a new home is a decidedly optimistic act for anyone. For Judit and Reinert Røksund, pushing ahead with the design and build of Villa R was not only optimistic but also therapeutic, given that the project overlapped with a challenging time for the family. The Røksunds and their two children had been living on one of the islands in the Bømlo district to the south of Bergen for many years when they found out that plans for a new road and bridge would have a significant impact on their existing home. Given that the family loved the setting and surroundings, the solution was to build a new house on a hilltop site further away from the road that also offered a mesmerizing open vista across the islands.

'I grew up in the area and my father also grew up in the old house just below where we are now,' says Reinert, an engineer working in the oil industry. 'I took over the house in the mid-nineties, but then the government told us they were building the new bridge and road in 2014. That was when we started fantasizing about building a new house and this plot of land on the hill caught our attention. The old house did not have much of a view but from here it's great and we face south-west, so we get the evening sun now. But it was a huge step to take.'

Over two or three years the family agreed to sell their former property to the government and bought the site for the new house, as well as beginning to work out what they wanted to achieve with the design of the new building. The Røksunds started drawing up a detailed list of what they needed and thinking about an architect, so that by the time the first conversations began with Todd Saunders they had already established a clear brief.

'We had lived in the old house for fifteen years and our children had grown up there, so that gave us a clear idea of what we wanted in the new house,' says Reinert. 'We made a functional spec that we gave to Todd because it was really important to us that the house functioned really well for us, as well as being a beautiful building. With Todd, we both liked the work that he had done previously and his way of expressing himself, and he had some really interesting proposals when he came to see us with these two distinct parts of the building connected by the staircase. The ideas that Todd had in mind worked with the site really well and were easy and functional.'

As an experienced engineer himself, Reinert decided to manage the construction process as a self-build project. But then Judit, a school teacher, fell ill with cancer and their plans were thrown into question while she began a course of treatment. They decided to press ahead with the new house, seeing it as a positive step forwards into the future for the whole family.

'I told Reinert, coming out of the doctor's office, that no matter what happens we will build this house,' says Judit. 'I wasn't really able to be part of the building process because I was having treatment by then, but the drawings and dreams were exciting. We had a dream of building something for a long time, and when we got married I said that we should build our own house one day. So I was happy whenever I felt well enough to be part of it and it was both fun and exciting for me, even if it was exhausting to make decisions when I was undergoing treatment. But I don't know if I would have done anything differently, apart from taking more part in it, if I had been well enough at that point.'

Previous pages – The new house adopts a prominent position at the top of the hillside, overlooking the water below; at the same time, it seeks to place itself positively and sensitively within the landscape, tucked among the trees and the topography.

Opposite – Model-making and site analysis sought to explore the relationship between the new villa, the land and the coast; importantly, the house adapts to the natural contours of the site rather than demanding that nature adapt to architectural tectonics.

"The design of the house maximizes the potential of the hilltop site, while working around the rugged topography as it dips away towards the water below.

— DOMINIC BRADBURY

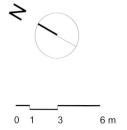

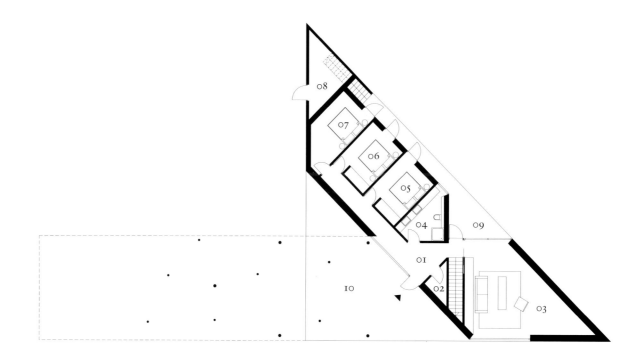

GROUND FLOOR

01 Entrance
02 Technical room
03 TV room / Living room 2
04 Bathroom
05 Bedroom 1
06 Bedroom 2
07 Bedroom 3
08 Storage
09 Covered terrace
10 Covered entrance

1ST FLOOR

11 Entrance
12 Garage
13 Laundry / Storage
14 WC
15 Bathroom
16 Master bedroom
17 Walk-in wardrobe
18 Office
19 Kitchen
20 Dining room
21 Living room
22 Covered terrace
23 Terrace

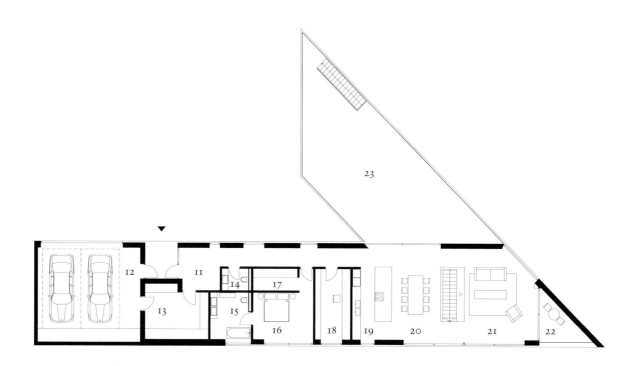

Pages 222–27 – The angular form of the house gives it a dynamic and characterful quality, yet at the same time the villa adapts to the folds and shifts of the hillside setting; in this respect it offers a balancing act between contextual synergy and sculptural innovation.

Above and opposite – Outdoor rooms and spaces are an important and integral part of the house as a whole, with the main living spaces feeding out onto a terrace situated upon the roof of the lower level and an undercroft below the 'bridge' formed by the elevated element of the house offering a more sheltered retreat.

'It was therapeutic for me too,' says Reinert. 'It was a kind of therapy to start the foundations and to do something. If we had made the decision not to sell the old house and not to do this, then we would have regretted it. The idea that we could experience living in this new house together became a motivation for me. It was a lot to think about, but I felt that I did have control of the project and that made me calmer, while the progress we could see brought us some brighter spots.'

For Saunders himself, the project took on fresh relevance and resonance. Working with clients on the design and build of a family house clearly involves a relationship that is both personal and professional, but here the project took on a new level of importance for all involved. The fact that Reinert was managing the construction process himself meant that the dialogue over details and design questions was also more direct than might otherwise be the case.

'When you design houses you do get really close to families and it is an intimate process,' says Saunders. 'You learn a lot about them and a lot about yourself as an architect. With Reinert and Judit, it felt like the project was really helping them by giving them a goal that they were heading towards together. It was about turning a difficult situation into an opportunity. My job as an architect is to make the process as positive as possible, which was very much the case with Villa R.

'When I first met Reinert I thought he was just like a Newfoundlander, because he can work with his hands and fix anything, so I had complete confidence in him and his ability to build the house. If he had a question then he would call me or I would drive down and we would sit down for an hour or two and solve everything. I really enjoyed working with Reinert in that way because he is very organized, very calm and they are both very optimistic people.'

The design of the house itself maximizes the potential of the hilltop site, while working around the rugged topography, including rocky outcrops and the mature trees that populate the sloping land as it dips away towards the water below. Much of the house is arranged on one principal level, including an integrated garage and storage room at one end, alongside the main entrance. Beyond this, a line of circulation passes the master suite and a dedicated study, both of which are orientated towards the view, before reaching an open-plan living space holding the kitchen, dining area and sitting room, with a covered terrace beyond. Saunders describes this space as a kind of 'rural penthouse', offering a framed panorama of the water, the trees and the neighbouring islands. The elevated position of the house means that this space, with its wall of floor-to-ceiling glass framing the vista, has the feel of a sophisticated treehouse or observation point floating above both land and sea. At the same time, a wood-burning stove forms a key focal point here and enhances the sense of warmth.

Previous pages – Saunders describes the main living area as a kind of 'rural penthouse': an enticing, elevated and open setting for appreciating the natural beauty of the surroundings.

Left and opposite – The white stairway forms a subtle line of separation between the seating area and the kitchen/dining zone beyond; the sitting room also connects with a sheltered balcony alongside it.

Following pages – The kitchen/dining zone leads out onto the morning terrace.

Pages 236–37 – Seen from the north-east, the two distinct elements of the house become clear, fusing together to create one larger home.

'I think of it as a hybrid space,' says Saunders, 'with this very rural, almost agricultural building combined with the sense of height and drama that you might have in a penthouse or a residential tower. It is an amazing position on top of the hill and that room makes the most of it. When you look out at the landscape, it's like a painting that's always changing.'

The main body of the steel-framed, timber-clad building forms a kind of bridge stepping over the lower portion of the site and spanning a sheltered undercroft that forms an additional outdoor room. One end of the bridge, around the garage and entrance zone, is supported by the rock outcrop while the other end is held aloft with the support of a modestly scaled lower level that pushes back from the rest of the house at an angle of ninety degrees. This lower zone holds a media room, as well as two bedrooms for the Røksunds' children plus an additional bedroom for guests.

This lower floor becomes, in effect, an annexe for the children, providing them with a private realm of their own that can be accessed independently from the rest of the house and also has its own covered terrace. Such an arrangement means that this part of the villa can, to a significant degree, function as a separate and self-contained space, if desired, for the children to use as they grow older. Just as importantly, the plan of the house means that all of the key spaces sit on the principal

storey with a fluid sense of connection between them.

'It's very simple and functional having everything on one level and also having the garage, store and laundry integrated with the house,' says Reinert. 'It's a big advantage compared to the old house, which was three storeys. The terrace facing west is such a nice place to sit in the afternoon, even when it's windy, because it's covered so we can still enjoy the view. We can slide the doors open completely and walk straight outside to the terrace from the living room.'

The thoughtful design of the house means that daily living becomes easier and more straightforward. The firewood store, for instance, is in the garage, meaning that the family don't have to go outside when they need more timber for the stove. For a family with a love of sailing, being able to change wet clothes in the store room and laundry alongside the entrance is also very practical. Such elements make everyday life more pleasurable.

'What I have come to understand is the importance of connecting with an architect who has a totally different perspective compared to our own,' Reinert says. 'We worked together to create the house that we wanted and it matured over time. But also, for us, finishing the house was a sort of victory on many levels because Judit fought through it all and is healthy and we finished the project. Everything turned out well.'

REFLECTIONS

Opposite – Like Villa S – Saunders' home near Bergen – Vassvika, his country cabin and farmstead at Lysefjorden, is a place for experimentation with new architecture, the adaptation of existing buildings and garden design. The site includes Library House, a hybrid yoga space-cum-vegetable garden and an old woodshed converted into a bathroom.

Experimentation & Innovation

A few years ago, in February 2016, Todd Saunders was skiing in Japan with friends when his group was caught in an avalanche. Saunders is an experienced skier and his team and guide were well equipped, but it was a dangerous and life-changing moment.

'I grew up in the snow, in Newfoundland, and I ski all the time in Norway, but nothing can really prepare you for an avalanche,' says Saunders. 'There was this blue light behind me and a big crack in the mountains with snow coming at us in a sheet that must have been one hundred metres wide. I could feel it and you think that you are going to be taken by the avalanche. It's the feeling that this is the end.'

Fortunately, Saunders was able to ski away from the path of the snow and two other skiers caught in the avalanche were dug out safely. But it was part of a significant process of reassessment, with the architect beginning to question what was important to him and the directions that his life, and his work, were taking him. Around the same time, Saunders reached the age of fifty, adding to the impetus to take stock.

'Around that time we had over thirty projects underway in fifteen countries, and I decided to stop and pause until I could get my core values in place and be true to myself,' says Saunders. 'I started to feel that I was living life in a certain way because other people had convinced me that it should be that way. So I said no to anything new for six months and took some time to really think about the kind of work that I wanted to do while making sure that I was true to myself.'

After the trip to Japan, the decision-making process took on a fresh level of importance, with more time taken to consider the kinds of projects that Saunders and his practice wanted to devote themselves to. Saunders also decided to devote more time to personal projects, recognizing the value of self-generated buildings such as his own home in Bergen, Villa S (see page 192), which serve as laboratories for developing fresh ideas.

Following on from Villa S, Saunders acquired a rural smallholding or farmstead, known as Vassvika, for himself and his family to the south of Bergen. Situated by the water at Lysefjorden, this collection of cabins and huts allows Saunders another fresh opportunity to explore new and experimental thinking. These include both new structures and conversions of existing buildings, as well as hybrids such as a yoga terrace that works around the existing trees while also incorporating beds for vegetables and other planting.

'A couple of architects visited me at the cabin recently and compared it to Alvar Aalto's Experimental House at Muuratsalo in Finland [1952],' says Saunders. 'It's that idea of having a personal testing ground, which is what Vassvika has become for me. It's a combination of old and new, with some buildings from the 19th century that we have updated and adapted, along with the new things that we have done here. It's somewhere that I have freedom to explore materials or make furniture or design a garden. Architecture is usually about slow cooking and you have to wait a long time to eat your meal. But here, I can put something in the oven and take it out and eat it right away. I love the immediacy of it.'

Other plans for Vassvika, which already accommodates seven buildings, include the conversion of an existing cabin into a ceramics workshop and the creation of a new office and work studio in the boathouse, which will give Saunders the option of working from home out in the countryside.

'It's a testing ground where nothing is really set in stone or pre-determined,' Saunders says. 'I hired my daughter to research outdoor bath tubs the other day, for instance, because it could be a great idea for here. Next year I'd like to build a greenhouse and a chicken house. We have a pond that we might use for keeping some fish or crabs and we have done some courses here, too, on kayaking and foraging. Maybe we will run some courses for architects as well and aim to do something once a month, as a way of teaching more informally.

'For me, it's a place to experiment and fill in some of the gaps and holes in my own knowledge. There's no separation here between work and living and taking time out – it's fully integrated. Just sitting in an office all day doesn't really work and there are times I need to be outside and working with my hands, or just sitting quietly for a while and drawing. Vassvika gives me those opportunities.'

‘For me, it's a place to experiment
and fill in some of the gaps and holes
in my own knowledge.

— TODD SAUNDERS

Design Ambitions – Small

At the same time, the compound nature of Vassvika, with its collection of small and complementary structures, fits with some of the design themes that Saunders has been exploring over recent years. A number of the practice's residential projects, such as Lily Pad (see page 84) and Salt Spring (see page 56) in Canada, as well as Villa Tyssøy (see page 156) and Villa AT (see page 68) in Norway, consist of two or three separate structures with a master building complemented by a separate annexe that might serve as a guest house or work space. Importantly, creating a small compound of modestly sized buildings helps to reduce the impact of these structures on the surrounding landscape, while also providing separate escape pods for work or leisure.

At Fogo Island in Newfoundland, Saunders famously developed a family of separate artists' studios that he has described as small 'punctuation marks' on the land and coast. Again, these are modest, sculptural retreats that both respect and frame the surroundings. Here, too, the escapist character of these buildings and their relative isolation act as spurs to creativity of all kinds. For the future, Saunders hopes to have his own rural retreat on Fogo Island for himself and his family, offering a way of spending more time in Newfoundland, where he grew up, as well as another personal architectural testing ground.

An interest in micro-structures, studios and cabins has led Saunders to develop his own concept for a prefabricated studio that can be made in a workshop and then delivered to site. Saunders recently completed the first full-scale prototype, known as XS ('Xtra Small'), with plans in place for a handful of additional sizes. The prototype can be loaded onto a lorry and delivered to a site for installation, making it a convenient and tempting option even for relatively isolated rural locations.

'The little projects that we do often help inform the larger projects,' says Saunders. 'For example, we are doing a large visitors' centre in Maine but have tried out a few ideas in Norway already. With the prefabricated studio, or cabin, the idea is not mass production but something we can build in a workshop to our design in a controlled environment. The weather here in the winter can get really rough, so the idea of having our carpenters working inside on one of these makes a lot of sense.

'It's a live/work unit that you could use as a small cabin or for work or as an artist's studio. Or it could be a yoga studio or something like that or you could have a collection of them to use for vacations. We do get a lot of calls about doing studios and small buildings, so this gives us a model where we can design, build and install something that's adaptable enough to be used in different ways.'

Design Ambitions – Large

At the other end of the spectrum, the practice is taking on larger, more ambitious and complex projects in different parts of the world. The Fogo Island Inn and associated projects on Fogo Island, such as the recent Fogo Island Shed, which is used as a stand-alone dining pavilion, took Saunders and his team to a fresh scale of ambition and complexity. The Fogo Island Inn has attracted the attention of many new and prospective clients.

'Fogo was a project that was about tourism, landscape and philanthropy,' says Saunders. 'Similarly, our new project in Maine combines those elements, and the Aurland Lookout brought together tourism and nature. We like working on these larger projects, which bring together these different elements and we are shifting more in that direction.'

The practice has also, over time, become more selective about the house commissions that they take on. As seen throughout this book, their residential work is usually seen as a collaborative process shared with clients who are imaginative, creative and often entrepreneurial. Larger-scale residential projects such as Carraig Ridge in Canada, similarly, tend to exist within the context of a meeting of minds.

Property developer Ian MacGregor fell in love with the area around Carraig Ridge, which sits alongside Banff National Park, as a child when his parents bought a cabin here. He has been coming back ever since. Helped by his success in the energy business, he began buying up parcels of land around the family ranch to make sure that the area would never be over-developed or environmentally compromised. Over time, the family has assembled a holding of around 6000 acres, with around 650 acres given over to the new community of Carraig Ridge, which will eventually host just forty-four houses.

MacGregor and his daughter Kate, a trained architect who is also involved in the project, selected a small number of architects to design the first houses at Carraig Ridge. They include Jim Cutler, who designed the much-lauded Rock House here; Tom Kundig of Olson Kundig; and Todd Saunders, who designed a 'family' of five houses for this unique rural development.

'You could almost describe it as a 650-acre park or natural preserve,' says Saunders. 'It's between Calgary and Banff so not too far from either city, but you have great cross-country skiing, hiking, mountain biking, horseback riding – you are in the middle of this incredible rural escape. From the work that we had done before, Ian saw that we would have a sense of responsibility and stewardship for the land when we were making architecture here. For me, seeing that Ian and Kate had also chosen Jim Cutler and Tom Kundig, who are both architects that I looked up to when I was at architecture school, was a real honour.'

The MacGregors have established a clear design philosophy for Carraig Ridge based on this idea of stewardship. Their model of 'integrated conservation and development, superior design and community experience' means that each house has plenty of space to breathe within a protected landscape, while the infrastructure of the community is maintained and looked after by the family's development company. Architecturally, the MacGregors wanted to aim for 'timeless' designs that have a harmonious relationship with their surroundings.

'I do have this belief that we are only the temporary custodians of the land, so we should be doing the best job that we can with it,' says Ian MacGregor. 'In a way, what we are doing isn't about the houses because it's about the place, so the buildings have to respect what's there and not dominate the landscape. Kate really convinced me that we should aim for contemporary architecture, so what we tried to do was look for the best people that we could and things that we both like.

REFLECTIONS

'What we liked about Todd was that he really cares about the design intent and what a building will look like when we're done. He wants things done to a high standard and has a vision, but he will also let us figure out the best way to build it that we can, which is something that we know quite a lot about. So that's the kind of working relationship that we will default to in the future.'

Finding that they had much in common beyond a shared love of the landscape, Ian MacGregor and Saunders began an ongoing dialogue about ideas and designs for a series of houses at Carraig Ridge. Saunders started work on a handful of site-specific designs for five locations identified by the MacGregors, which were carefully mapped and documented. Architect and client agreed on the need to preserve the existing landscape as far as possible, working around the trees and vegetation while ensuring that each residence could enjoy a healthy degree of privacy, balanced with the need to connect with the surroundings and the views. The first of these five houses, the Y House, has recently been completed, with others to follow.

'Todd and I are very similar,' says Ian MacGregor. 'He will listen to what we want and he will try and put his own configuration on it. There is some back and forth on design ideas, but he will give us a fair amount of rope because he knows that we won't drive it over a cliff. He also understands that if you cut something down, if you alter the landscape, then it will never get back to the way that it was in your lifetime. We really spend a lot of time thinking about that and making sure that the trees are marked and recorded. We can never replicate what took ten thousand years to create.'

Previous pages – The Fogo Island Inn, on Fogo Island in Newfoundland, has established itself as a destination hotel; Saunders' design fully respected the precious ecology of the setting while maximizing connections with the landscape and the coast.

Above – The Carraig Ridge commission, near the Banff National Park in Alberta, Canada, involves the design of a series of houses that are site-specific and fully respect and respond to a unique landscape.

Opposite – Such site-responsive work is at the heart of Saunders' design ethos, with his buildings adopting the lightest of touches upon the landscape and finding synergy with the natural surroundings.

Architecture, Nature & Respect

An ingrained respect for the natural world and the environment connects all of Todd Saunders' projects together, whether small, medium or large. This also lies behind the practice's decision to be more careful about the kind of projects that they commit to in the future, while ensuring that their clients share similar values and concerns.

The environmental impact of any building, whether it's a micro-studio or a larger development, is taken very seriously. Saunders also recognizes the opportunity to take the same kind of environmental principles exhibited in his one-off houses to larger communities, while exploring net-zero and self-generation energy options.

'Off-grid can be pushed much further and Scandinavia and Canada are the perfect places to do it,' says Saunders. 'Developing micro-communities that are entirely off-grid is a really interesting challenge in itself. In a way, it's going back to where I started out as a student with my thesis looking at green villages in Northern Europe. Planning and designing a community for fifty families would be a step forwards for us and really interesting in terms of the opportunities and the economies of scale. It's the modern equivalent in some ways of a garden village, and another way of thinking about living with the natural world while looking after it at the same time.'

For any architect, it is important to take some time now and again to reflect upon their own work and their direction of travel. Working on this book has allowed me just such a golden opportunity. Looking back over the practice's residential work from the last few years, I have come to appreciate that we have – for some time now – been asking some important questions about what house and home are really for, while blurring boundaries between spaces devoted not just to daily living but also to creativity of all kinds, including cooking, growing, entertaining, working, writing and reading.

In this respect, we have never seen houses simply as 'machines for living'. Over the years I have come to appreciate how much our clients' lives are shaped and touched by the houses and buildings that we design and build for them. For an architect, there is no other kind of commission that is quite so personal and intimate. In any truly successful residential project the client becomes a creative partner, playing a vital part within an inclusive and collaborative team, while we – as architects – always try to remember that this is their house and not ours.

I'm also struck by how important it is to take your time to realize a truly successful and rounded project. As a young architect I was always impatient for the next commission, but I have come to understand what Leo Tolstoy meant when he said that 'the two most powerful warriors are patience and time'.

To design and build a great house takes us between one and five years, but that's just as it should be and understanding the correct time-frame for such a significant creative process is one of the most important elements of an architect's career.

Conversely, we also need to maintain a sense of momentum in our work. Inevitably, one project should inform the next as we perfect ideas and carry thoughts and themes forwards, but without ever repeating ourselves or becoming a one-trick pony. There is a very careful balancing act here, as I hope this book has suggested, between evolution and originality.

One of the most important of these themes has been the exploration of hybrids of all kinds. An artist's studio, for example, is not just a studio but a shelter, a micro-home, a belvedere, an observatory and a refuge. Similarly, our houses might incorporate a yoga studio or a gym, a sauna, a boathouse, a guest house, a workshop, a library and perhaps an office or a business of some kind. Increasingly, such projects encompass more than one piece of architecture and become a compound, or a version of a modern farmstead. This inevitably results in a family of separate but interrelated structures with communication between them, and the message we take is that this is much more than a house. These are the kinds of themes that will continue to preoccupy us, as we continue to ask what houses are for and how they should be designed.

Todd Saunders.

CREDITS, BIOGRAPHIES, AWARDS
& ACKNOWLEDGMENTS

PROJECT CREDITS

Villa Austevoll (p. 18) Kalvaneset, Austevoll, Norway

Architects: Todd Saunders with Pedro Léger Pereira and Attila Béres

Builder: Blænes Bygg

Other consultants: GG Møbel and Erling Olsen – Konstruksjonsteknikk AS

Villa S+E (p. 40) Bergen, Norway

Architects: Todd Saunders with Attila Béres and Pål Storsveen

Interior architect: Claesson Koivisto Rune (CKR)

Garden and landscape architect: Anleggsgartner Ellingsen AS v/ Olvar Ellingsen

Builders: Framtidsbygg AS and Walløe & Nilsen AS

Other consultants: Kvassheim Elektro AS

Model maker: Monika Jasioková

Salt Spring (p. 56) Salt Spring Island, British Columbia, Canada

Architects: Todd Saunders with Ryan Jorgensen, Attila Béres, Ken Beheim-Schwarzbach

Interior architect: Nancy Krieg

Garden and landscape architect: Nancy Krieg

Builders: Gord Speed, Cyrus VanOort, Rob Wilson, Adam Milner, Bob Akerman

Other consultants: Greg Slakov, Jim Helset

Villa AT (p. 68) Søgne, Norway

Architects: Todd Saunders with Attila Béres, Márk Szőke, Joshua Kievenaar and Joseph Kellner

Interior architect: Hannes Wingate

Main building contractor: Øyvind Bakkevold

Interior carpenters: Stig Frange and Helge Ingebretsen

Lily Pad (p. 84) Muskoka, Ontario, Canada

Architects: Saunders Architecture with Pedro Léger Pereira, Attila Béres, Matt McClurg and Márk Szőke

Architect of record: Matt Ryan (FAD Architects)

Interior architects: Studio Author Interior Design

Garden and landscape architects: Holbrook & Associates Landscape Architects, Rockscape Landscapers

Builders: Thomas McConell, Tonnel Construction/ Earl Ferguson Construction/Shell

Villa Grimseiddalen (p. 102) Bergen, Norway

Architects: Todd Saunders with Pedro Léger Pereira, Matt McClurg, Maxime Rousse and Attila Béres

Builder: Nilsen og Andersen AS

Electrical and lighting: Bergen Elektro Automasjon AS

Kitchen and wardrobes: Kvanum

Kitchen appliances: Gaggenau, Audio and image: BEA Lyd & Bilde AS

Bathroom: Flis & Murmesterforetning AS

Fireplace: Gassmannen AS

Villa Refsnes (p. 138) Bergen, Norway

Architects: Todd Saunders with Pedro Léger Pereira, Pål Storsveen and Sofia De Sousa Pacheco

Interior architect: Stine Homstvedt (SCH Design)

Garden and landscape architect: Tommys Hage

Builders: Mads Holm Bygg & Prosjektering AS

Other consultants: Georg Guntern, GG Möbel AS

Villa Tyssøy (p. 156) Bjørøyhamn, Norway

Architects: Todd Saunders with Ken Beheim-Schwarzbach and Matt McClurg

Interior architect: Todd Saunders

Garden and landscape architect: Todd Saunders

Builder: Hilleren Prosjektering

Other consultants: Jarle Johannessen, Drømmekjøkken/ Multiform/Gaggenau/Alape/Minde Snekkeri/Dinesen

Villa Grieg (p. 170) Bergen, Norway

Architects: Todd Saunders with Pedro Léger Pereira, Attila Béres, Pål Storsveen and Ricardo Coutinho

Interior architect: Jonas Evensen

Garden and landscape architect: Ragni Helweg

Builder: Mats Holm Bygg og Prosjektering AS

Supervisor/plumber: Trond and Lars Erik Ravneberg and Odd Hansen

Electrician: Arild Rygg

Engineers: Erling Olsen – Konstruksjonsteknikk AS, Knut Rødland

Villa S (p. 192) Bergen, Norway

Architects: Todd Saunders with Ryan Jorgensen, Chris Woodford, Attila Béres, Márk Szőke and Pedro Léger Pereira

Interior architect: Hannes Winsgate

Garden and landscape architect: Todd Saunders

Builder: HSR Bygg AS

Engineers: Erling Olsen – Konstruksjonsteknikk AS

Villa R (p. 218) Mosterhamn, Norway

Architects: Todd Saunders with Pedro Léger Pereira, Maxime Rousse, Márk Szőke and Attila Béres

Interior architect: Jane Dunkley, In Design

Garden and landscape architect: Saunders Architecture

Contractors: Sunnhordland Bygg AS, Nils Morten Ådnanes, Arild Lillenes

Model maker: Monika Jasioková

BIOGRAPHIES

TODD SAUNDERS is one of the most important contemporary Canadian architects working internationally. Saunders, who has lived and worked in Bergen, Norway, for the past twenty-five years, has executed projects in Canada, Norway, the USA, Sweden and Finland, creating simple yet powerful architecture with a strong sense of northern identity informed by the natural landscape. Today, Saunders combines teaching with practice. His current focus is on architecture and art projects that seek to instigate change and give back to local communities.

DOMINIC BRADBURY is a writer and journalist specializing in architecture, interiors and design. He has written over thirty books, including many titles for Thames & Hudson such as *The Iconic House*, *The Iconic American House*, *Mid-Century Modern Design* and *New Nordic Houses*. As a freelance journalist, Bradbury contributes to many newspapers and magazines in Britain, the USA and internationally, including *The Times*, *The Financial Times*, *The Observer*, *House & Garden* and *Wallpaper**. He lives in Norfolk, England, and is a visiting lecturer at the Victoria & Albert Museum, London.

AWARDS, HONOURABLE MENTIONS, JURIES, PUBLICATIONS

AWARDS AND HONOURABLE MENTIONS

2020

Royal Canadian Academy of Arts, Inductee

GRAY Awards, Gold Winner – Fogo Island Shed, Commercial Architecture

WAN Awards, Gold Winner – Fogo Island Shed, Leisure

2019

Dezeen Awards, Longlisted

Platinum A' Design Award, Winner – Architecture, Building and Structure Design

Golden A' Design Award, Winner

2018

National Geographic Society Unique Lodges of the World – Fogo Island Inn

Condé Nast Traveler Readers' Choice Award – Fogo Island Inn

2017

Travel + Leisure World's Best Awards – Fogo Island Inn

2016

Honorary Doctorate of Fine Arts from Nova Scotia College of Art and Design

Municipality of Bergen Architecture Prize, Nominee

AR Emerging Architecture Awards, Shortlisted

Architizer A+ Awards Jury, Winner – Fogo Island Artist Studios

Architizer A+ Awards, Finalist – Fogo Island Inn

2015

enRoute Hotel Design Awards, Winner – Best Overall Architecture

DesignCurial 'World's 10 Best Public Toilets' Award, Winner

AZ Social Good Award, Winner

2014

ArchMarathon Award, Milan, Italy, Winner – Workspace

PURE Awards, Shortlisted – Pure Life Experiences

The Hotel and Property Awards, Shortlisted

MCHAP for Emerging Architecture, Nominee

Culture Trip – 'Contemporary Norwegian Architecture: The 10 Best Buildings of the Last Five Years'

Travel + Leisure – 'It List' of the Best Hotels of 2014

Condé Nast Traveler – Hot List

Hospitality Newfoundland and Labrador – Accommodator of the Year

Architectural Digest – Fogo Inn: one of the 'Ten Most Daring Buildings in the World'

AFAR, The Experimental Travel Awards, Winner

2013

TIAC National Cultural Tourism Award, Winner

Travel + Leisure Global Vision Award, Winner – Culture

enRoute – 'Canada's Best New Restaurants 2013'

2012

Tatler – Style with Soul Award, Winner

*Wallpaper** – Best Public Project, Nominee

2011

Huffington Post – '5 Greatest Architects Under 50'

Municipality of Bergen Architecture Prize, Nominee

Arnstein Arneberg Award for Outstanding Architecture, Winner

HISE Award for Sustainable Excellence, Winner

AZ Best Commercial Building Award, Winner

2010

ArchDaily Building of the Year, Nominee – Culture

2009

BauNetz – '100 Best Architects in the World'

BO BEDRE – '10 Best Architects in Norway'

New Norwegian Blood – 'Top 10 Architects Under 40'

2007

*Wallpaper** – Best Public Project Prize, Nominee

2006

Norwegian National Construction Prize, Winner

Mies van der Rohe Prize (European Union Prize for Contemporary Architecture), Nominee

AR Emerging Architecture Awards, Honourable Mention

Condé Nast Traveler – one of the 'Next 7 Architectural Wonders of the World'

2004

Young Norwegian Architects – '20 Under 40'

2000

Norwegian National Artists Scholarship
– 3 years

Kvam Herad Environmental Prize for
Ålvik Schoolyard, Winner

1995

Canadian-Scandinavian Travel
Scholarship

American Institute of Architects Research
and Special Studies Scholarship

JURIES

2021

Eurasian Prize

2020

Volume Zero Tiny House Architecture
Competition

2018

Western Living Magazine,
Designer of the Year

Young Architects Competition:
Military Museum, Sardinia, Italy

2017

New Zealand Home Awards

2016

Governor General's Award, Canada

2015

Alpitecture, Meran, Italy

Norwegian National Construction Prize

2014

Environmental Architectural
Competition, Norwegian Association of
Architects, County of Hordaland, Norway

Norwegian National Construction Prize

2013

Norwegian National Construction Prize

AZ Awards, Canada

Hiše Award, Slovenia – Innovative
Excellence, Sustainable Excellence

2011

Jury Leader, Norwegian National Prize
for Architecture Students

enRoute Hotel Design Awards

Design Competition for the 75th
Anniversary of the Stavanger Architecture
Association

2008–2011

Norwegian Annual Concrete Prize

2008

Form Magazine Scandinavian Architecture
Prize

2005

Living Design, Finland

PUBLISHED IN

Monocle

DETAIL

Domus

Mark

Vogue Living

Dwell

Condé Nast Traveler

Arkitektur N

Nytt Rom

Wall Street Journal

Icon Magazine

AIT

Concept

ELLE Decor

enRoute

Häuser

D2

Arkitektur DK

Room

Wallpaper*

Azure

Architectural Digest

IW Magazine

Beaux Arts Magazine

L'Architecture d'Aujourd'hui

Dagbladet

BO BEDRE

Form

PICTURE CREDITS

All plans and drawings are provided courtesy of the architect. Please note that the numbering system used on the plans resets at each floor level, jumping to the next available digital sequence; ground-floor rooms, for example, begin at 01, while first-floor rooms begin at 11 or 21 and so on.

The following credits apply to the photography for which separate acknowledgement is due:

2 Bent René Synnevåg; 3–6 Ivar Kvaal; 11 Bent René Synnevåg; 13 (top) Nils Vik; 13 (middle and bottom) Bent René Synnevåg; 15–19 Ivar Kvaal; 20 Todd Saunders; 22–39 Ivar Kvaal; 40–41 Bent René Synnevåg; 42 Todd Saunders; 46–55 Bent René Synnevåg; 56–57 C.J. Berg; 58 Todd Saunders; 60–65 Ema Peter Photography; 66–67 C.J. Berg; 68–69 Bent René Synnevåg; 70 Todd Saunders; 72–83 Bent René Synnevåg; 84–85 doublespace photography; 86 Todd Saunders; 88–101 doublespace photography; 102–03 Bent René Synnevåg; 104 Todd Saunders; 106–19 Bent René Synnevåg; 122 (top left) Todd Saunders; 122–23 (top right) Bent René Synnevåg; 122 (middle and bottom) Todd Saunders; 124–35 Todd Saunders; 138–39 Bent René Synnevåg; 140 Todd Saunders; 142–57 Bent René Synnevåg; 158 Todd Saunders; 160–69 Bent René Synnevåg; 170–71 Ivar Kvaal; 172 Todd Saunders; 174–91 Ivar Kvaal; 192–93 Bent René Synnevåg; 194 (top left) Ryan Jørgensen; 194 (top middle, top right, second row, bottom left, bottom right) Todd Saunders; 194 (bottom middle) Astri Sangolt Saunders; 196–211 Bent René Synnevåg; 211 Iwan Baan *St George's Church in Lalibela, Ethiopia*; 212–17 Bent René Synnevåg; 218–19 Ivar Kvaal; 220 Todd Saunders; 222–37 Ivar Kvaal; 240–42 Bent René Synnevåg; 245 (left) Iwan Baan; 245 (top right) Alex Fradkin; 245 (bottom right) Bent René Synnevåg; 246 Mir Visuals; 247 Bent René Synnevåg

ACKNOWLEDGMENTS

I would like to thank all of the people who have been involved in this book and in the creation of each of the projects presented here. There are many people to thank but unfortunately I'm only allowed to write five hundred words and it would take pages to thank all of you. I am forever grateful for each and every one of your collective and individual contributions, ideas and patience, and for the time that we spent together during this ride. It has been fantastic.

I would especially like to thank my two daughters, Sina and Astri, who pop up in photos in this book on numerous construction sites and unusual locations. My architecture has given us so many opportunities, allowing us to meet many spectacular people and travel to some unique places. I hope that these houses and projects will inspire each of you, as you follow your own path, and will help you to live life to the full.

I would like to thank all the architects, junior architects, interns and other staff who have worked with us over the years. Thank you for everything that you helped us with. In particular, I would like to thank three architects in my studio who have been involved with these projects as far back as fifteen years ago. Thank you to Attila Béres, Ryan Jørgensen and Pedro Léger Pereira; all three of you taught me so much and I appreciate the times that we have had together and I look forward to seeing your lives unfold in a great and wonderful way.

Thank you to Dominic Bradbury for the enjoyable conversations we have had every Thursday over the past year. I imagine and hope that we can continue with other projects as we both grow older.

Finally, I probably don't know a lot of you, but thank you for reading this book. I really do appreciate that you have taken the time to look through these pages and have shown interest in our work. My father shared something valuable before he passed away about making the world a better place, in that he always talked to strangers, echoing the poet William Butler Yeats's belief that a stranger may well be a friend that you haven't met yet. So, maybe one day we will meet. I hope you all enjoy what we have made and understand that all of it was hard and honest work, made with care, thought and patience.

Author's acknowledgments

Dominic Bradbury would like to express his sincere thanks to Todd Saunders and his colleagues, particularly Tone Fondevik, as well as to the many clients and homeowners who kindly offered their valuable time and thoughts about their new northern houses. Grateful thanks are also due to Ian Holcroft, John Jervis and all of the team at Thames & Hudson, especially Fleur Jones, Lucas Dietrich, Evie Tarr, Rosie Coleman Collier, Jane Cutter and Helen Fanthorpe.

First published in the United Kingdom in 2021 by
Thames & Hudson Ltd, 181A High Holborn, London WC1V 7QX

First published in the United States of America in 2021 by
Thames & Hudson Inc., 500 Fifth Avenue, New York, New York 10110

For a full list of picture credits, see page 254

Designed by Ian Holcroft

British Library Cataloguing-in-Publication Data
A catalogue record for this book is available from the British Library

Library of Congress Control Number 2021934222

ISBN 978-0-500-34368-5

Printed in China by RR Donnelley

MIX
Paper from
responsible sources
FSC® C144853

Be the first to know about our new releases,
exclusive content and author events by visiting
thamesandhudson.com
thamesandhudsonusa.com
thamesandhudson.com.au